THE JOURNEY

From Ideation to Business

LAW ACCENT

Published by:
Heart2World Publishing
info@heart2worldpublishing.org

For information on distributions, translations, or bulk sales,
please contact
LAW ACCENT

CONTENT

Acknowledgment

We owe it to God for the privilege given to us to achieve this feat. Our goal is to not just set standard for the legal industry but to redefine what it means to be a legal practitioner. I will continue to reference the quote of Christopher Williams Sapara that the legal practitioner lives for the direction of his people and the advancement of the cause of his Country.

I am grateful to the Law Accent team. It started with Joy Abina-we won together at the very early beginning of Law Accent. Adedamola Abe who has been a pillar in the firm exercising patience from the first day she joined the firm (not just patience to learn but also to earn) and she has continued to believe in the vision of the firm while also growing with it. Precious Ibanitoru has also been fantastic. Couple of works referred to in this book would not have been possible without his involvement. His passion for the field of intellectual property is amazing and I am sure he would continue to find a home in that field no matter what he opts to explore. Segun Awoyinfa, the tech savvy lawyer that drives the Firm outside of its comfort zone to ensure we remain tech driven and also build on that which we already know. Damilola Kolawole too has been awesome; takes little or no supervision for her to achieve results. Our support team that helps us to be in sync; Tomi Duduyemi, Henry Nathaniel and Wande Olutuyi. You guys are great and it has been a wonderful experience working with everyone. Big thanks to Mr. Olaniyi Gbolahan for accepting to write the preface to this book. His support has been unwavering over the years.

I must also appreciate my darling wife, Obasola Ogunyemi, for all the support. She welcomed my undying love for law from day one and has never denied me a place at her side for all the times I was out with my second love.

I also appreciate The Accent SMEs Hub; a community of entrepreneurs who gave us the mandate to always come back every weekend to teach from our knowledge reserve. Without them, we may never have been able to put together this book.

The one thing that has driven Law Accent until now is our passion to serve and we will continue to focus on that as we forge ahead to the next chapter of our being as a people.

Eyitayo Ogunyemi
Managing Partner, Law Accent

Preface

I started doing business about fifteen years ago. I had no entrepreneurial training of any kind, trained as an Architect, all I had was a bundle load of passion and a desire to succeed. I made a lot of mistakes and more than a few were avoidable.

Navigating the rudders of business in Nigeria has many challenges, but the journey can be somewhat easier when one is thoroughly prepared through hindsight and mentorship. If you are just about to start a business or you already just started a new enterprise, how would you register the new entity? Do you know what type of incorporation is best for your goals or is business partnership for you? How do you protect yourself if the business fails? How do you handle tax? How do you protect your trade secrets or enter into contractual agreements with vendors? How do you recover debts or enforce a contract? I haven't even asked about preparing contractual agreements with employees and landlords or how to sustain your business and ensure it continues to grow and hopefully one day, your succession plan comes into play.

I will not beat about the bush. You need this book. I wish I had the good pleasure of reading it 15 years ago. It is always better to avoid mistakes by learning from the wealth of experience of others. You will save yourself immense pain and loss and many businesses have completely failed because they had no idea about all of the priceless knowledge taught in this book.

The Journey (Ideation to Business) is a well written, foolproof compendium of much of everything an entrepreneur who is starting in business needs to know and to be candid, even those who have been in business for a while. It simplifies the journey of entrepreneurship for the non-legal reader, enough to help you understand how to properly navigate your startup through its growth process to major success.

I encourage you to make this a textbook, read it as many times as necessary. Be sure to leave it on your desk so you can refer to it when you need to. Gift it to friends and family who are starting up in business and be sure to not just read it but implement all of the ideas that Law Accent has put into this immensely needed book.

Olaniyi Gbolahan
GMD, GOA Group

CHAPTER ONE

BUSINESS STRUCTURING

STARTING LINE: DECIDING THE KIND OF REGISTRATION FOR YOUR BUSINESS

N igeria is a free enterprise country. Doing business is therefore acceptable except there is a law that says otherwise.

In most cases, where a business is prohibited or regulated, it is usually so because the business is sensitive and it is in the best interest of the nation that the business is prohibited or regulated. You can therefore participate in any form of business within the bounds of the law. This chapter discusses the different options of registration that you can do for your business and the differences between those options.

In starting your journey as an entrepreneur in Nigeria, there are different registrable business options. The Companies and Allied Matters Act which was signed into law in 2020 expanded those options such that an entrepreneur can choose from a wider range of options. Below are the realistic options that you can choose from at the starting line of your business:

- Business Name
- Limited Liability Partnership
- Limited Partnership
- Incorporated Company

FACTORS THAT AFFECT CHOICE OF REGISTRATION

There are certain factors that should guide your choice of registration. Some of these factors include; the nature of the business you want to establish, the available capital and the number of people involved in executing the idea, whether you would like a limitation to the liabilities or involvement of company co-owners and the sphere of operation that you are considering, to mention a few.

Sometimes, your target customers might also affect the kind of registration. For instance, foreign persons, multinationals and some government agencies prefer to do business with incorporated companies because of the sentiment that incorporated companies' accounts are audited every year and form part of their public records. That way, there is a little chance of falling into the hands of "fly by night" businesses.

Another factor is if there is a law that mandates a specific form of registration for a line of business. For instance, it is a requirement of the law that a person who intends to do the business of money lending can only register an incorporated company.

In some cases, the cost of registration might impact your decision, it may even be about pre-registration requirements and compliance needs. For instance, if you want to operate in the banking and finance industry, you will need approval from the Central Bank of Nigeria and your business cannot operate in the industry if it is registered as a business name.

Your own desire also matters. What exactly do you want? A man goes to a car lot, considers the cars there and decides on the one to purchase based on the value of his pocket, the realities of the road, the expertise of his driver and his personal choices.

You therefore need to consider these factors among others before you start your entrepreneurial journey.

REGISTRABLE OPTIONS AVAILABLE FOR YOUR ENTREPRENEURIAL JOURNEY

A BUSINESS NAME

This is otherwise known as a trading name. It is the name or a style by which a business is carried on.

Business name registration is the cheapest form of registration. It does not require payment of stamp duties or share capital charges. After starting business, it is relatively easier to understand the tax and other compliance frameworks for business names.

The option of registering a business name is best suited for those whose primary reason for wanting to register their business is because of their desire to do business in a name other than their natural names. Doing business is inherent to our being as humans, that is why we presumably do not need anybody's approval to do business. However, for the need to ensure public protection, the law mandates that when you start a business in a name different from your natural names, then, you need to register that name. In essence, "Frank Olawale Bayero" does not need to be registered if the person that bears the name is the one doing business. But if it is "Frank Olawale Bayero & Co." there is a need to register having added something to the name.

The requirement to register any trading name which is different from one's natural names is a good practice particularly when viewed from the fact that it protects the user of the name and also protects the public. No doubt, you would love to have the monopoly of right to any business name that is approved for you.

In a similar vein, it helps the public to be able to identify the person(s) using a name to do business to reduce the chances of fraud among other reasons. So, the law mandates registration for the protection of the public as much as for your own protection and safety.

A Business Name does not have a life of its own distinct from the owner(s). This is because it is the name that the law seeks to protect and not the entity. It therefore means that the business is not a person (i.e. artificial person) under the law; you cannot buy property in the business name, you generally cannot sue or be sued in the name and it cannot be a party to an agreement without the owner(s) being stated in the agreement. Except where a law permits it to do any of the points stated, it generally cannot do those things.

If you are starting a sole proprietorship or a partnership, having your business registered as a business name is one of the ideal options that you have.

A sole proprietorship is a one-man business. It revolves around the entrepreneur alone and all decisions, liabilities and profits rest on the entrepreneur.

A Partnership is a form of arrangement between people and not necessarily a form of business registration. Someone once said partnership is two or more partners in a ship. If your decision is to register a business name for your partnership, you cannot start with more than 20 people, else you need to register as an incorporated company or start a limited liability partnership.

There are very limited circumstances where more than 20 people are allowed to register as a business name. They are:

- Partnership of more than 20 lawyers
- Partnership of more than 20 accountants
- Cooperative society.

INCORPORATED COMPANIES

Incorporated Companies are profit oriented entities registered by at least one person. They are also referred to as "body corporate", "artificial persons", "corporate entities" and so on. All of these qualifications are because, unlike a Business Name, Incorporated Companies have a life different from their founders, they have legal personality and can sue or be sued.

There are six types of Incorporated companies that you can register in Nigeria:

1.   Incorporated company limited by shares
2.   Incorporated company limited by guarantee
3.   Unlimited company

Any of the three registration options can either be a Private or Public company depending on factors which include whether you want to be able to freely invite members of the public to invest in your idea and you want to do so through public platforms (including the Nigeria Stock Exchange).

A public company limited by shares may be listed to transact its shares on the floor of the Nigeria Stock Exchange such that it sells its shares to members of the public. It could even go on air, television, radio, newspaper, to invite members of the public to buy its shares. This is different from private companies limited by shares which can only solicit for purchase of its shares privately from people without engaging public media.

A private company limited by shares may be registered by one person and may have up to fifty shareholders. For the purpose of numbering the shareholders, those who own shares jointly are considered to be a single shareholder and shares owned by employees and former employees who had gotten ownership from the period of employment are not counted among the Fifty.

"Limited" "Unlimited" "Guarantee", etc. are qualifiers used to explain the limitation of an incorporated company.

"Limited" means there is a limitation. "Limited by shares" means that the liabilities of members are limited to the amount unpaid on their respective shares.

"Limited by Guarantee" means that the members' liability is limited to such amount as each member respectively undertakes to contribute to the assets of the company if the company is wound up. In essence, members come together to guarantee that if something goes wrong during the lifetime of the company limited by guarantee, they each guarantee to contribute the amount stated against their respective names in the company's registration documents. It is for this reason that a company limited by guarantee ought to be used for objects which are not-for-profit in nature instead of full-fledged commercial ventures. Objects which the law recognises can be started with a company limited by guarantee include to promote commerce, art, science, religion, sports, culture, education, research, charity or other similar objects.

While a company limited by guarantee can do business, that must not be the core of its existence. When it does business, the profits cannot be distributed among its members. Its income and the properties of the company must be used solely for the promotion of what the company is established for. If you therefore want to start a purely commercial venture, a company limited by guarantee may not be your best option.

An UNLIMITED Company as the name goes is a company where the liabilities of members have no limit. Even though the company has a separate legal personality, any member of the company may be called upon to settle the liabilities of the company individually and to any extent. For that reason, it is not a commercially viable option to invest in.

It is common to equate "company" with "incorporated company", but those two do not mean the same thing. A "company" could be registered as a business name but when a company is "incorporated", that word is a technical word used to represent any of the three options highlighted above (limited by shares, limited by guarantee and unlimited companies).

LIMITED LIABILITY PARTNERSHIPS

Limited liability partnership is one of the inventions of the Companies and Allied Matters Act, 2020. Two or more persons who wish to carry on a lawful business in Nigeria with a view to profit can now form a limited liability partnership as a legal entity independent of its partners.

Upon registration, the partnership becomes a body corporate which is capable of suing and being sued, it can own properties in its name and have a common seal.

You need at least two partners to form a limited liability partnership. While individuals and corporate bodies may be partners in a limited liability partnership, you will need to have at least two individual persons who will act as designate partners (i.e. involved in day-to-day operations). It is a further requirement that at least one of the designate partners must be resident in Nigeria.

While members of incorporated companies have most of their duties, roles and privileges spelt out in the Companies and Allied Matters Act, articles of association and shareholders agreement, a limited liability partnership is mostly regulated by partnership agreement signed by the partners and lodged with the corporate affairs commission.

The option of business name registration is available to a maximum of 20 partners but a limited liability partnership can accommodate more partners and the death of a partner does not nullify its existence especially where there is or are prospective partners seeking to subscribe to the partnership agreement which forms the basis of the limited liability partnership.

LIMITED PARTNERSHIPS

A limited partnership as a form of registration is similar to a business name in that it can accommodate a partnership of not more than 20 persons. However, it differs from business name in that there is a need to have at least one general partner and one limited partner to form a limited partnership. The phrase "general" and "limited" are used to describe the extent of liability and responsibilities of each of the partners. In essence, a general partner is responsible for the day to day operation of the partnership and may have an unlimited liability for the debts of the business, while a limited partner is one whose liability in the partnership is limited to the extent of the partner's investment or promise in the business.

A limited partner is barred from participating in the management of the firm and lacks the capacity to bind the firm by his/her actions. If the limited partner decides however to be involved in any operation, the partner will be responsible for any liability that arises from the specific operation as though a general partner.

If your intention is to engage in a business as a passive partner or an investor, one of the ideal options that you may explore is limited partnership. That way, you may contribute funds for a stake in the business while you do not have to be involved in the day-to-day affairs of the business. You may by yourself or through an agent of your choice inspect the accounting records of the business at any time so as to know the state of the partnership and advise the partners on it.

Where a partnership is not registered as a limited partnership, it is deemed to be a general partnership, so if your intention is to start a limited partnership, you must ensure that details of the arrangement are stated in your registration document. The details meant here include the details of the general partners and those of limited partners, sum contributed or agreed to be contributed by each limited partner, and so on.

PRACTICAL ANALYSIS OF THE DIFFERENCES BETWEEN BUSINESS NAME, INCORPORATED COMPANY, LIMITED PARTNERSHIP AND LIMITED LIABILITY PARTNERSHIP

This crucial question is discussed extensively in the next module. However, below are the basics:

1. Registration: Business name registration is easier to set up compared to the other registration options. As of the time of publishing this book, the basic things needed for business name registration after name approval include: company email and address, details of owner(s) which should include two passport photos, means of identification, email address, residential address and phone contact.

For an incorporated company (using a private limited liability company as an example), you need to supply details of director(s), shareholder(s), secretary (if any), objects of the business, memorandum and articles of association (i.e. the constitution of the business), etc. For a limited partnership, you need to provide the company email and address, details of general partners and those of limited partners, terms on which the partnership is entered (if any), a statement to confirm that the partnership is limited, the sum contributed or agreed to be contributed by each limited partner, etc. For a limited liability partnership, the details of the partners need to be supplied alongside the designate partners information and partnership agreement (if any).

2. Formation: Business name may be formed by one person (sole proprietor) and may not have more than twenty people. A private limited liability company may be formed by one person, it can have up to 50people as shareholders and even more in some circumstances. A limited partnership may be formed by between two to twenty persons while a limited liability partnership may be formed by two or more persons.

3. Separate Legal Personality: If you are doing business as a

business name operator or a limited partnership, your entity will not be considered as a separate business personality; it cannot even sue or be sued in its name so it is more ideal to sue the owner or partners directly. Conversely, incorporated companies and limited liability partnerships have separate legal personalities from their members or partners, so they can be sued or even sue in their respective names.

4. Liability of members: Liability of sole proprietors or partners doing business as a business name is usually unlimited because the business revolves around the sole proprietor or partners as the case may be. If you operate a private limited liability company, liability is according to the extent of your shareholding in the company. Liability of limited partnership depends on whether the partner is a general partner or a limited partner. While the liability of a limited liability partnership is born by the entity itself subject to certain exemptions.

5. Issuance of shares: Business name generally does not issue shares upon registration. On the other hand, co-owners of an incorporated company have their stake expressly stated in the company documents. The stake of business name owners is usually not stated in company registration papers, the ideal thing

therefore is for them to have their stakes stated through private arrangement like a partnership agreement or some form of registration under State laws. In the case of a limited liability partnership, the rights and duties of the partners ought to be stated in the partnership agreement to be lodged with the corporate affairs commission. While the extent of contribution of partners in limited partnership is ideally supposed to be stated in its registration documents.

6. Administration: All decisions made by the proprietor are independent of any form of opinions since it is a one-man business. The same thing is obtainable in a single member limited liability company. Conversely, partnerships are regulated based on what is contained in the partnership agreement. For incorporated companies and limited liability partnerships, decisions are made by the board of directors and partners respectively through resolutions.

7. Meetings: Some of the meetings of incorporated companies are provided for by law, business name, limited partnership and limited liability partnership on the other hand do not have meetings mandated, provided or regulated by law.

8. Dissolution: Dissolution of business name is easier compared

to other registration options. You do not need a crowd of officials to officiate when you decide to quit and "bury" the remains of a business name, but that is not the case for incorporated companies in particular which need special officials to play different roles; the accountant, tax practitioner, auditor, lawyer, receiver, liquidator, etc. These by implication make incorporated companies more expensive to part with. In the case of a limited liability partnership, dissolution could be voluntary or by the court.

CONCLUSION:

The choice of registration is probably one of the most important decisions to make when starting your entrepreneurial journey. When you make the right decisions, it positively affects everything about your business.

Now that you know the different registration options, we would, in the next module, guide you on practical things you need to consider in making a decision on which registration option to choose at this critical phase of your entrepreneurial journey.

Practical Guides to Choosing Between a Business Name, Limited Partnership, Limited Liability Partnership and Private Limited Liability Company

Introduction:

In this module, we would look at practical points that should shape your decision on which option to go for if you are stuck on choosing between a business name, limited partnership, limited liability partnership or a private limited liability company.

As a recapture, an entrepreneur with interest in operating a commercial business in Nigeria may operate as a sole proprietor or form a partnership. Either ways, the entrepreneur can register a business name or incorporate a company (i.e. Incorporated Company). Where the entrepreneur's sojourn is with another person(s), the additional options of limited partnership and limited liability partnership comes into play.

When an entrepreneur aims to operate a business that revolves solely around the entrepreneur, then he or she must be thinking of operating a SOLE PROPRIETORSHIP. In essence, the benefits and liabilities revolve around the entrepreneur alone.

Sole proprietorship is the easiest business structure to form. Nevertheless, it does not mean that it cannot grow to become a business empire. A ready example is the DANGOTE story. According to a report, as a start-up, Aliko Dangote operated as a sole proprietor, so that it was once the joke in financial cycles that Nigerian bank CEOs prayed first thing every morning asking God to grant Dangote good health, for if the good Alhaji kicked the bucket, not a few banks would have crashed under the weight of debt gone bad, if not toxic.

A sole proprietor can register as a business name or a private limited liability company under the Companies and Allied Matters Act.

'Partnership' on the other hand may be considered as two or more people that come together to paddle a business. In a more formal sense, 'partnership' is used to describe the arrangement between people and not necessarily the type of registration that was done for the business. That is why partners may choose to register any of the registration options available under the Nigerian law.

One of the questions that we usually ask our executive business students during training sessions for entrepreneurs is for them to explain what they understand by an Incorporated Company, and a Business Name, and why they will choose the business option that they are opting for. Unfortunately, we rarely receive an answer that captures the basic differences, and it is unfortunate too that many founders and investors have chosen their business options without proper guidance.

Furthermore, with the introduction of limited partnership and limited liability partnership, it is essential that you understand how they operate so that you can make a well-informed decision on which one to go for.

Below are keynote differences between a business name, limited partnership, limited liability partnership and an incorporated company in Nigeria. The points stated below are not exhaustive, but they constitute some of the basic differences that you will find helpful in deciding which one to register:

DIFFERENCE NO 1:

DO YOU WANT YOUR BUSINESS TO BE YOU OR DIFFERENT FROM YOU?

Business Name and Limited Partnership: A Business Name is a name and style with which you trade; it is just a 'style', and it is therefore not different from the owner. Being a mere style, the business does not generally assume a separate legal entity, cannot sue, nor be sued and properties cannot be purchased in the name of the business.

Another point that can be identified with the above is that when the owner dies, the business also dies (since in the first place, it does not have a life of its own).

The same thing applies to Limited Partnership which is more of an arrangement between two to twenty people who desire to qualify each person's roles. It therefore does not assume a separate legal entity as well.

Incorporated Company and Limited Liability Partnership: The moment an Incorporated Company or limited liability partnership is registered, it becomes a separate entity different from the founder(s). It becomes otherwise known as an 'artificial person'. The best way to understand this severance process is to consider pregnancy, and the delivery process - once a child is born, the child has an independent life; can grow, stand-alone (with time), and even die. The process of the growth of the child is not hinged as such on that of the mother.

By implication, 'your company' is considered to be different from you after registration; the co-owners may be broke while the company is rich, and the death of the founder does not necessarily mean the death of the company because the company has a life of its own.

DIFFERENCE NO 2:

DO YOU WANT TO START YOUR ENTREPRENEURIAL JOURNEY AS A SOLE PROPRIETOR? BUSINESS NAME AND INCORPORATED COMPANY (LTD) ARE YOUR GO TO OPTIONS

Business Name and Private Limited Liability Company: A Business name and Private Limited Liability Company may be registered by one person (sole proprietor). The Companies and Allied Matters Act 2020 now allows for single membership private limited liability companies (LTD) and that is good news for you if you wish to operate as LTD. By implication, you can have full control of your business while the company maintains the status of an artificial person which is capable of owning properties in its name.

Limited Liability Partnership and Limited Partnership: These arrangements demand that you operate together with at least one other person. They are therefore unsuitable for sole proprietors.

DIFFERENCE NO 3:

DO YOU WANT THE VALUE OF YOUR INVESTMENT IN THE BUSINESS TO BE PUBLICLY ACCESSIBLE? EVERY OTHER REGISTRATION OPTION (EXCEPT BUSINESS NAME) WILL DO THE MAGIC

Incorporated Company, Limited Liability Partnership and Limited Partnership:

If your level of ownership, stake, investment, or interest in your proposed business differs from that of your co-investors and you want this to be recorded publicly, you may choose to start a private limited liability company, limited liability partnership or a limited partnership.

Business Name: If you register a business name, your level of ownership, stake, investment, or interest will not be publicly recorded. If for any reason you prefer to register a business name and you want the extent of your ownership, stake, investment, or interest to be clearly spelt out, you can do this by preparing a memorandum of agreement between you and your partners. You may consult a business advisory law firm to help you with the agreement.

DIFFERENCE NO 4:

DO YOU WANT TO REGISTER A BRAND THAT YOU CAN USE TO INVEST IN OTHER BRANDS? PRIVATE COMPANY LIMITED BY SHARES (LTD) AND LIMITED LIABILITY PARTNERSHIP WILL DO THE MAGIC

Private Company Limited by Shares and Limited Liability Partnership: If you want to register a special purpose vehicle that can serve the purpose of being a shareholder or a partner in other entities, your go-to options are LTD or a Limited Liability Partnership. LTD will be most applicable if you intend to operate alone while you may choose between LTD and Limited Liability Partnership if it is a partnership.

If you are a foreign investor with a company already registered in your country, you must ensure that your existing company is capable of owning shares in the new company to be registered in Nigeria. You do this by ensuring that your existing company has legal personality.

If the existing company is however undergoing a process of being wound up, it cannot join in the formation of the company to be incorporated.

If you want to use your existing company to own a stake in a Business Name, Limited Liability Partnership or Limited Partnership, you can give instruction to your legal consultant to list the existing company as a partner in the new Business Name to be registered.

Business Name and Limited Partnership: You cannot use your business name or limited partnership (as an entity) to own shares in a company.

DIFFERENCE NO. 5:

IF YOU HAVE MORE THAN 20 PARTNERS, YOU MIGHT JUST HAVE TO INCORPORATE A COMPANY OR REGISTER A LIMITED LIABILITY PARTNERSHIP

Incorporated Company and Limited Liability Partnership: Where a business is intended to be carried on as a partnership, and the partners are more than 20 people, the business can either be registered as an Incorporated Company or Limited Liability Partnership but not as a business name or Limited Partnership because the latter entities permit up to twenty partners but not more.

You can register the following three businesses as a business name notwithstanding that the partners are more than twenty:

Co-operative Societies registered under any law in Nigeria:

A partnership of more than 20 lawyers each of whom is qualified to practice as a lawyer in Nigeria. Or a partnership of more than 20 accountants each of whom is qualified to practice as an accountant.

Where the total number of persons who intend to own the shares of a proposed company is more than 50 people, the company may register as a public company. In other words, a private company in Nigeria must not have more than 50 shareholders.

As explained in the earlier module, private companies may have more than 50 shareholders in some situations. For instance, where an employee becomes a member/shareholder upon his employment, or where the employee continues to be a shareholder during and upon the expiration of his employment, he may not be counted for the purpose of numbering the 50 members.

Consider the following illustrations:

If AZ LTD has 50 shareholders and Bob was given a number of shares in AZ LTD upon his employment, he is not going to be numbered as Number 51 shareholder; rather, the number of shareholders will still stand at 50 in the eye of the law.

In a similar vein, if Bob continues to hold shares as an employee until he stops working for AZ LTD, and he continues to own the shares after his employment, he is not going to be numbered for the purpose of counting the fifty (50) benchmark.

Two or more people, even an Association or a Group can invest in a company jointly. They are treated as a single member for the purpose of numbering the members of the company. It is however important that the Association or Group must have been registered under the appropriate law.

Conversely, there is no limitation to the number of persons that can come together to form a limited liability partnership.

DIFFERENCE NO. 6:

THE STATUS OF YOUR KEY INVESTORS DETERMINES THE KIND OF BUSINESS ARRANGEMENT

Incorporated Company: In an Incorporated Company arrangement, the shareholders are considered as the joint owners of the company. The shareholders elect the board of directors who are responsible for the daily affairs of the company and also give a periodic account of management to the shareholders.

Note however that a shareholder may also be a director or even the company secretary.

Business Name: Unlike incorporated companies, there is no clear-cut difference between the business owner and the director in a business name arrangement. This is because in most cases, the role of the director is played by the owner of the business.

Limited Partnership: A stakeholder in a limited partnership arrangement is either a limited partner or a general partner.

Limited Liability Partnership: In this arrangement, the stakeholders are referred to as partners among whom are designate directors who are in charge of the day-to-day operations of the business.

CONCLUSION:

The difference between a Business Name, Limited Partnership, Limited Liability Partnership and an Incorporated Company is broad and can be viewed from different perspectives.

However, the details covered in this module form the basics that every entrepreneur must take cognisance of in making decisions on what choice of registration to opt for. In the next module, we will discuss the realistic structuring approach if your intention is to start a partnership.

REALISTIC STRUCTURING APPROACH FOR PARTNERSHIPS

Introduction:

Partnerships are on the increase across the globe for an obvious reason, which is that it creates room for shared knowledge, expertise and resources which in turn has the prospect of leading to better products and services. In this module, we will consider your entrepreneurial journey as a partnership and guide on key things you need to note to have a smooth ride with fellow partners.

Let's start with the basics. A partnership is the coming together of two or more people to start a business for the aim of profit-making.

In broad terms, there are three types of partnership:

General partnership: This involves two or more people forming a business with a common goal to make a profit. The partners may identify role play from the beginning of the journey but they have a joint responsibility for the success or otherwise of the business. When they win or lose, make profit or loss, moments are shared together equally. Even the decisions made by one on behalf of the company are considered to be made by all and bind all in equal proportions.

Limited partnership: A limited partnership comprises at least one general partner and one limited partner. If you have a limited partner in your business (or if you probably are the limited partner), it means that the limited partner has a limited personal liability, unlike a general partner. A limited partner might sponsor the business journey but may choose not to be actively involved in the operations. In essence, the limited partner often is a silent partner, contributing money to the business without being involved in the running of the partnership business.

Limited Liability Partnership (LLP): Just like the option of limited partnership, the Companies and Allied Matters Act 2020 now allows people to register a Limited Liability Partnership. Unlike a general partnership, where every partner in the firm is liable jointly with other partners for all debts and obligations of the firm, a partner in a limited liability partnership is not liable for the debts, action or inaction of the partnership beyond the amount subscribed by the partner under the partnership agreement. The limited liability partnership as a special genre of vehicle has a legal personality as it can sue and be sued in its registered name. A partner in a limited liability partnership may however be liable to be sued in the partner's personal capacity for acts of the partnership in the event of fraud, misrepresentation, and other improper conduct alleged to have been committed by the partner.

If you are looking to journey as a partnership, it's important to spell out what each person contributes, such as finance, property, service, client referral, and what each person expects in terms of profits and ownership. The best time to talk about the terms of partnership is just before the journey begins. Each partner should know their individual roles and all. It is a good idea to work out the 'what ifs' which are probable and foreseeable as well.

Partners should decide in advance who is getting what, who is doing what, who is responsible for what, how to resolve disagreements and what happens if a partner wants to pull out of the journey (retire or resign) or if one partner wants to expand and the other does not.

Partners may also orally agree on terms of the partnership; it is however recommended to put the terms down in writing.

REGISTRABLE OPTIONS

Partners need to agree on the type of registration for the business.

Where partners are between 2 and 20, they are at liberty to opt for either a business name, limited partnership, limited liability partnership or an incorporated company. However, for a partnership of more than 20 people, the two realistic options are limited liability partnership and incorporated company.

Here are some critical elements to agree on before the journey so as to have them stated in the partnership agreement:

1. Roles and contributions of Partners:

Each partner's contribution to the formation and financing of the business should be agreed upon and spelt out at the earliest time before the journey begins. This will include subjects such as how much each partner contributes to starting the business and each partner's responsibilities such as what each partner will contribute, not only in the amount of money but also concerning time, effort, customers, equipment, etc.

2. Profit and loss distribution.

This is one aspect of partnership that should be carefully considered when starting your partnership journey. Partners are in the business to make a profit. It is, therefore, necessary to agree on the partners' distribution percentages reflecting their share of partnership profits and losses. Where this is not stated, the assumption is that the partners have equal stake in the business even though partners' contribution differs.

3. Management:

Partners need to agree on whether or not all the partners would be involved in the management of the partnership; they need to decide what each person is to do. If the partnership agreement is silent on role play, then it may be assumed that all the partners will be involved in management.

4. Remuneration

Partners need to decide whether or not there will be remuneration for the partners and the structure of remuneration if any. We start journeys to get to our destination and both the vehicle and drivers ought to be catered for in the course of the journey. The natural assumption is that partners are entitled to remuneration except if the partnership agreement states otherwise.

5. Voting rights of partners, bringing new partners onboard, and general administration and management.

Partners need to define how day-to-day management and long-term decisions will be made. Who gets the last say? What types of decisions require a unanimous vote by partners, who should be at the key driving seat of the business and what decisions can be made by a single partner?

If the partners are able to have a clearly mapped decision making structure before starting their journey, it would help to avoid delayed decision making, unhealthy rivalry, and would aid the smooth running of the business.

6. Dissolution of the partnership.

Another important thing to mutually agree on when considering a partnership is the question of how to opt out. Partners should agree before the journey on how any partner that wants to exit can do so. The peak excitement period of a business journey (other than when the business is growing healthy and fast) is just before the journey; at this time, the energy level is usually high, optimism too is high and chances of failure are shelved. Sometimes too, a journey may be planned for a precise time or purpose such that once the time or purpose is actualised, the journey can be said to be over. Partners should therefore agree on the circumstances under which partners can withdraw, the length of notice they must provide, and how the assets will be distributed.

The dissolution clause in the Agreement may also deal with other issues such as, what happens if one partner retires, relocates, goes bankrupt, becomes disabled, or dies in the cause of the journey. It should provide for limitations of partners upon exit. For example, relationship with customers or a prohibition from doing similar business in the same geographic area as the partnership.

7. Dispute management mediums.

What happens where partners have disagreements during their journey? This does happen and that is why it is essential to include in your partnership agreement how disagreements will be addressed. You may want to specify that partners go for mediation, arbitration, conciliation, direct to court, etc. It can also be included that while parties agree to explore out-of-court settlement, such agreement will not hinder a person from going to court to seek for an interim relief. The nature and peculiarities of the business should be considered in choosing a dispute management approach.

JOURNEY AS A FOREIGN PARTICIPATOR

I n this chapter, we will address the question of whether, and to what extent, a foreign national or alien can participate in business in Nigeria. A foreigner is any person that is not a Nigerian Citizen. "An alien" is a person or association, whether corporate or incorporated, other than a Nigerian citizen or association.

What if you want to have a business journey with a foreigner? Can a foreigner participate in forming a company with you in Nigeria? What if you are not a Nigerian but desire to do business in Nigeria, can you? The simple answer is "yes!". So far it is done within the bounds of the law, an alien or a foreign company may join in forming a company in Nigeria. The same principle applies if you are the foreigner seeking to do business in Nigeria. You may choose to journey as a business name operator, limited partnership, limited liability partnership or an incorporated company considering the factors discussed in earlier modules.

If you are a foreign company that wants to do business in Nigeria but maybe not for the long term or if you seek to do business without registering your company in Nigeria, the ideal thing would be to apply to the office of the Minister of Trade for exemption from the need to register.

Regulatory Authorities on Foreign Participation in Nigeria

If you are a foreigner or you desire to have a foreigner as a partner, you will need to process certain types of permits, approvals and licences. Without those approvals, it might be somewhat impossible for a foreigner to do business or register a business organisation in Nigeria especially if the foreigner intends to be actively involved in the day-to-day operations of the business in Nigeria.

The agencies that you might need approvals from include the Corporate Affairs Commission responsible for the registration of corporate entities, the Nigerian Investments Promotion Commission that regulates and promotes investment activities and the Nigeria Immigration Service that regulates the entry of foreigners into the country amongst others.

Modes of Participation

There are two ways for foreigners to participate in Nigerian businesses.

Foreign Direct Investment – A foreigner that wants to start a business journey in Nigeria may register a company. The foreigner may even join as a co-owner of an existing company through a merger or an acquisition.

Foreign Portfolio Investment – A foreigner may desire to just support the journey with capital through capital importation. In essence, if an alien wants to invest in the shares of a company, whether public or private, he can do so through Foreign Portfolio Investment.

What if you are a registered foreign company that wants to do business in Nigeria?

It is desirable to register your foreign company in Nigeria where you decide to start an entrepreneurial journey in the Country. It is however not mandatory in some cases.

Steps to take for Foreign Direct Investment

- Obtain, from the Nigerian embassy, the appropriate visa subject to regularisation for owners and officers of the company.

- Secure an address in Nigeria for receiving documents and other pre-formation correspondence of the company.

- Prepare and execute joint venture agreement and other pre-incorporation contracts if in partnership with Nigerian(s) or other foreigner(s).

- Incorporate the company with CAC and obtain the original certificate of Incorporation and other documents.

- Import capital through an authorised dealer (i.e. approved bank) and obtain a certificate of capital importation issued by Central Bank of Nigeria.

- Register the company with the Nigerian Investment Promotion Commission.

- Apply to the Securities and Exchange Commission (SEC) for registration of interest of foreigners in the shares of the company.

- Obtain relevant permits from the relevant regulatory agencies. For example, if your line of business involves capital exchange, you might need approval from the Central Bank of Nigeria

Apply to obtain relevant incentives and reliefs available for foreign investors in Nigeria.

Importation of Capital through Foreign Exchange

A foreign investor wishing to buy shares or import foreign capital/loan for doing business in Nigeria should freely import the capital through an authorised dealer, which currency is convertible into the Naira at the official foreign exchange market. This is provided in the Foreign Exchange (Monitoring and Miscellaneous Provisions Act)

Procedure

- This can be done by buying Nigeria debt instruments abroad from any Stock Exchange at a discount rate.

- A Certificate of Capital Importation will be issued to the Foreigner.

- The foreign company/investor will then present the CCI-

Certificate of Capital Importation to the Central Bank of Nigeria through authorised dealers, usually banks.

- The CBN will pay the face value of the Certificate of Capital Importation in naira.

Advantages of using Certificate of Capital Importation (CCI)

- It enables the opening of foreign currency domiciliary accounts with Banks in Nigeria

- Open a special non – resident Naira Account.

- Buy shares in Nigerian companies out of the naira account.

- It aids repatriation of capital, dividends and incomes without restrictions at autonomous market rates minus taxes.

- Unconditional transferability of funds through an authorised dealer in freely convertible currency.

- The company will be exempted from money laundering investigations.

- If the purpose is to finance foreign loan; the company will be allowed to purchase foreign currency at the official rate for the servicing of the foreign loan.

A foreigner can be a director, limited partner, general partner, designate partner or participate as a shareholder. It is also possible to participate in dual capacity. However, a foreigner who wants to occupy the position of managing director or designate partner must obtain a work and resident permit before he can do that.

Foreign nationals and entities may register and fully own shares of a company in Nigeria except for some statutory exceptions. For instance, at the time of publishing this book, companies seeking to bid for contracts in the oil and gas sector are required to have 51% of their shares owned by Nigerians.

CREATIVE WAYS TO PROTECT YOUR FOUNDER STATUS IN BUSINESS

Founding a business is a huge task. It demands a lot of intellectual efforts, time and money. This is why many entrepreneurs are usually emotionally attached to their startup.

Knowing how to structure your business and protect your stake as the business expands is a skill that you must know. You may not continue to have a hold on the business as it grows because it takes a community to raise a child. In essence, you (as the founder) may need to open up the business to third parties for their involvement so that the business can grow and remain healthy.

In this module, we would guide you on how to remain relevant in your company thereby protecting your founder status in the business.

(1) Register some of the company's intellectual property in your name

Regardless of your line of business, there is usually something to protect; it could be a recipe, formula, know-how, logo, information, etc. You may opt to protect them in your name and then license them to your company. This is best done before bringing in any investor and it should form part of your negotiations with the investors. Offer your company to investors but not your intellectual property.

It pays to own a literary, musical or artistic work (excluding photographs) in your name because the protection would last for a lifetime and 70 years thereafter, but if your business is to own it, it would only last for 70 years from the end of the year the work was first published. You will learn more about protecting your intellectual property in chapter six.

(2) Own Majority Shares

Own at least 51% of the company shares (directly or indirectly). That way, you have majority ownership.

Considering that the concept of non-voting shares is alien to the Nigerian corporate system, your interest is best protected if you opt to have majority shares.

Sometimes, investors do not like the idea of a founder having issued shares that cannot be justified. One of the things you can do is to make your stake vest within a period. In essence, if the company's total unit is 1,000,000 and you intend to own 500,000 units, you could vest it within 4 years so that you own 125,000 at the start while you work to earn the remaining shares.

Founder's vesting arrangements need to be structured with caution so that the founder is protected in precarious situations including where the company is sold before shares are fully vested and where co-shareholders are at loggerheads on whether the founder merits vesting of his/her shares, etc.

It is now a mandatory requirement of law that every annual return filed by an incorporated company or limited liability partnership must disclose details of any person with significant control of the company. This therefore needs to be taken into consideration when you fully earn your stake in the business.

(3) Have Founder's Privileges

"Founder's privilege" is a special right, advantage or immunity granted to a founder. Such rights may include voting rights, non-dilution of shares without consent, right to unaudited books of the company, right to attend board meetings, appoint a designate director, etc. The rights you can legally have will depend on existing laws and regulations, particularly corporate governance codes, so you should invest in understanding those laws and codes.

One of the ways to bring all these privileges together is to have them stated in the company's shareholders agreement and ensure that your company's articles of association are in tune with the agreement.

(4) Do the valuation of your contribution

As mentioned earlier, investors are usually keen to understand why you own what you own in the business, so it is in your interest to keep records of your contributions. This includes assets, equipment, manpower and finances. If you will actively resume day-to-day on the business, the best option is to put reasonable value to your services as well. Where the company is unable to pay salaries for your day-to-day involvement, you may opt for equity or have it as a convertible debt.

(5) Minority Protection

As the company continues to grow, there would arise the need for fundraising. One of the ways to raise funds is to offer company shares for some funds. The more rounds of funding are done, the more likely it is for a founder who was a majority shareholder at the beginning of the company to become a minority shareholder.

There is therefore the need to include the appropriate minority protection clause in the shareholders agreement, that way the interest of the founder is preserved.

(6) Prepare for life after you (i.e. share transmission)

Ensure that both your articles of association and shareholders agreement allow you to transfer part or your entire stake to a beneficiary of your choice and that you can transmit your stake upon demise through your Will. Alternatively, you can own your stake as a joint owner with your key beneficiary so that ownership automatically devolves to him/her after your demise.

(7) Be a Director

The Directors of a company are responsible for the day to day running of the affairs of the company. This means that they are in the loop of every activity in the company. As a Director, you have access to all financial and every other information. You may want to ensure you retain your directorship for as long as you have shares in the company.

(8) Build a Good Relationship with Investors

It is important for founders to build good relationships especially with investors. More so, who you allow into your business is critical to the success of the business. You will find some investors helpful as they play the role of both an advisor and mentor in some cases. As a founder, you therefore need to prioritise working with people you know and trust and ensure that you do a thorough vetting of personalities.

Conclusion:

As the company grows and takes on outside investment, the interests of the founders would in most cases diverge and this makes it necessary for you to protect your interests as the founder.

While there is no assurance that all the points above will be accepted by investors seeking to come into your business, they form a good starting point for your negotiation. You should bear in mind that your greatest leverage is hard work and knowledge of what you seek to achieve. If those things are available, it makes negotiation easier.

Whichever registration option that you decide to go for, you will find the ideas helpful and applicable.

Also, it may be advisable for you as a founder to seek separate legal counsel on how to protect your interests different from that of the company.

It is advisable to do this at the point of the formation of the company. This may be helpful to you at future points in the life of the company.

CHAPTER TWO

REGULATORY AGENCIES THAT MIGHT BE RELEVANT IN YOUR ENTREPRENEURIAL JOURNEY

CHAPTER TWO

Business is a journey and not a trip. Here, we will talk about some institutions that regulate your journey as you drive your business and pilot its affairs as an entrepreneur. An understanding of the roles of these institutions and their expectations from you will guide your decisions on how to navigate the road and know the red flags.

While some of these institutions and signs are applicable to all roads, some are applicable only to your chosen location, that is the path you have chosen to take.

There are various institutions and agencies set up by the government to regulate businesses in Nigeria. They are saddled with the responsibilities of administering laws, ensuring compliance and enforcing these laws, some of these agencies are established to issue licences and business operation permits just as the vehicle licensing office issues vehicle licence which will qualify your vehicle to freely move on the road.

Some of these institutions are generally applicable to all businesses irrespective of the sector or business objectives, some institutions, on the other hand, apply only to a particular field of business and regulations made are binding only on businesses within that sector. Each agency seeks to ensure that businesses carried on within the industry it regulates adhere to standards already laid down by the law.

We will briefly examine some of these agencies.

1.   The Corporate Affairs Commission
2.   The Federal Inland Revenue Service Commission
3.   National Agency for Food and Drugs Administration and Control.
4.   The Central Bank of Nigeria
5.   Standard Organisation of Nigeria
6.   Nigerian Communication Commission.
7.   Nigeria Immigration Service
8.   Nigeria Security and Civil Defence Corps.

The Corporate Affairs Commission (CAC)

The Corporate Affairs Commission is saddled with the overall supervision of all businesses in Nigeria irrespective of the industry. It is the first point of call for any business. It regulates the affairs of businesses from pre-incorporation, registration, commencement to closure of the business, etc. It supervises the formation, incorporation/registration, management and dissolution of businesses, and is also empowered to arrange and conduct investigation into the affairs of any company.

The commission also administers the law that regulates the general affairs of businesses and seeks to ensure strict compliance with the provision of the law. Your business, irrespective of the industry, is accountable to the corporate affairs commission. The agency has offices in different states in Nigeria to enable ease of access by business owners.

The Federal Inland Revenue Commission

This agency administers most of the tax laws in Nigeria except personal income tax which is managed by various State's tax agencies. The FIRS assess persons including companies, enterprises chargeable with tax, collects, accounts and enforce payment of taxes as may be due to the Government or any of its agencies and also collects, recovers and pays to the designated account any tax administered by it.

The agency in collaboration with the relevant law enforcement agencies, has the duty to carry out the examination and investigation of taxable persons with a view to enforcing compliance with the various tax laws. The agency maintains database, statistics, records and reports on persons, organisations, proceeds, properties, documents or other items or assets relating to tax administration including matters relating to waivers, fraud or evasion. It is the body that issues taxpayer identification number (TIN) to every taxable person in Nigeria.

It is saddled with the responsibility of collecting taxes such as Companies Income Tax, Value Added Tax, Petroleum Profit Tax, Capital gains Tax Custom and excise duties, stamp duty, education tax and other collections on behalf of the federal government, ensure and enforce compliance with tax laws as it applies to business.

National Agency for Food and Drugs Administration and control

This agency is saddled with the responsibility of regulating, inspecting, registering, issuance of certificate of quality and controlling the manufacture, sale and use of food, drugs, medical devices, chemicals, packaged water and drinks and importation or exportation, determine the suitability or otherwise of medicines, drugs, food products, cosmetics, medical devices or chemicals for human and animal use, conduct the necessary tests and ensure strict compliance with the standard specification in Nigeria.

Business owners whose products or business objectives require dealing in any of the services covered by the agency are therefore encouraged to understudy the agency, know the applicable regulations and ensure strict compliance with the laid down regulations. The agency has the power to punish defaulters and it can also initiate legal actions against defaulters.

The Central Bank of Nigeria.

The Central Bank of Nigeria is the apex and central body regulating the financial industries in Nigeria. This agency issues operation licenses to companies in the financial industry, regulates the inflow and outflow of legal tenders within Nigeria and also ensures strict compliance with laws regulating the industry.

Standard Organisation of Nigeria.

Just as the name implies, the agency is set up to administer standards for the production of goods, quality and fitness for purpose. The agency establishes standards specifications, quality control and metrology, designate and approve standards. It organises tests and does everything necessary to ensure compliance with laid down standards, undertakes regulations into the quality of facilities, systems, services, materials and products, whether imported or manufactured in Nigeria, it also evaluates quality assurance activities including certification of systems, products and laboratories throughout Nigeria.

It is vested with the responsibility of standardising and regulating the quality of all products in Nigeria. It regulates products quality by providing standards for products, measurement, materials and process of production and also regulates and registers all products manufactured, marketed, distributed and consumed in Nigeria. The agency is also empowered to impose fine and sanction defaulters.

As an entrepreneur who wants to deal in the production of household appliances and furniture, machines, etc., the Standard Organisation of Nigeria is the agency to reach for certification of the quality and standard of the desired product.

The agency has a compendium of standards for different

products and it is expected that there will be strict compliance with these standards.

Nigerian Communication Commission.

This agency regulates all businesses in the telecommunications industry, that is television and radio stations, mobile service providers, internet service providers, etc. in Nigeria. It also issues licences and ensures businesses are carried on in strict compliance with the laws.

Nigeria Immigration Service.

This agency controls the entry or exit of people in Nigeria. It administers residence and work permits to foreigners in Nigeria. Where your business requires that you engage an expatriate (foreigner) you are to visit this agency to process the necessary permits.

Nigeria Security and Civil Defence Corps.

The Nigeria Police is responsible for the protection of lives and properties of Nigerian and foreign residents in Nigeria. Irrespective of the existence of the Nigeria police and other established government agencies, some individuals and business establishments engage the services of private security personnel to watch over their properties.

In regulating the activities of these private security bodies, the Nigeria Security and Civil Defence Corps is empowered by law to issue licences, supervise and monitor activities of private security guards' company through its private guard company department.

Business owners who therefore desire to do business as providers of private security guards are to apply to the agency for license and also ensure strict compliance with laid down principles on how to manage the business without defaulting.

CONCLUSION

It is recommended that you consult a professional to advise on regulations and agencies regulating your chosen industry before you set up your business, as this will save you from the penalties for non-compliance.

Chapter Three

VALUING YOUR STARTUP

VALUING YOUR STARTUP

INTRODUCTION

Startup valuation is one of the most debated topics in the venture capitalist world. There are different schools of thought, various valuation methodologies, varying operating environments, amongst others, when it comes to the subject.

Whether you are at the idea level or already experiencing growth in business, you might desire to invite investors to pitch funds in your business idea. Sometimes too, your intention might be to merge with another business, buy the business or be bought by another business. These among other things would call for some form of business valuation.

This chapter addresses factors that affect startup valuation, how to value startups, the concept of term sheets and its components.

Let us start with key things that most investors consider before releasing money to startups:

KEY FACTORS THAT INVESTORS CONSIDER BEFORE FINANCING YOUR BUSINESS

Many conditions can sway investors to invest in your business, there are however two factors that stand out. They are:

a. A superior management/founding team.
b. An attractive product or service

Superior Management/ Founding Team: It is usually said that investors invest in people and not the business. This is true especially for businesses that are at the idea level or just starting out on their journey.

Having an idea does not equate having the quality to start up and operate the business. Therefore, to convince an investor to invest in your business, you and your board must be top notch in areas which bring value to the business. Your team must also be able to show the investors that the founders are committed to achieving the corporate goals and have committed not just time, but money, to the business. The easiest way to show this is to ensure that there is a vesting agreement. A vesting agreement is an agreement that shows that the founders have to earn rights of ownership by actively working in the company over a period of time.

You must also be deliberate about those you bring onboard the business. Who are your directors? Who are the shareholders? What are the professional qualifications of your company secretary? Bringing in family and friends simply for the sake of existing personal relationships or other forms of sentiments should be avoided and anyone listed in your company documents must be there for strategic reasons.

Attractive Products/ Services: A quality team with a poor product will render the whole business inefficient and unprofitable. The major factor that keeps a business afloat is what the business is able to offer to its target customers. Without an excellent product or service, the business may not be able to make money and investors may not be able to recoup investment.

Sometimes too, investors may be captivated by the ingenuity of your idea and the relevance of the service or product. If there is a high demand for your line of product, chances are that it would be easier to attract investors and your company valuation will rise.

MAJOR CONTRIBUTORS TO A COMPANY'S VALUATION

The Founding Team

This is a critical contributor to your valuation. As earlier stated, Investors usually love to be comfortable with the quality, execution ability, relationships and overall competence of the founder or founding team. This takes a toll on the valuation and the ability of the startup to raise financing.

Andela is a great example; the business is great but the quality of the founders is greater. Investors will trust their ability to execute and more importantly, create liquidity for them, sometimes in the future.

Previous Investor

There are some high-stake investors whose presence alone is sufficient to considerably boost the valuation of a startup company. In essence, your business valuation increases because of the prestige of the investors you were able to attract. This is why it pays to get quality investors early in your business journey.

Additionally, angel investors are good, but if you can get an institutional investor to support your business early on (even at a discount), you will reap the rewards in subsequent financing rounds.

Potential Investors

An experienced investor will always know whether or not a startup has lots of investors. The investor will factor in the other investors to determine the amount to commit, as well as the valuation.

Elite Liquidity Investor

This refers to a situation where there is a big investment by an elite investor that can provide liquidity to other investors. An elite investor is an experienced high-profile investor or participator in an industry. Where a giant investor invests in a business, it spreads fast to the public and creates curiosity among investors' networks. This may create positive or negative energy around the business and should be managed well.

HOW TO VALUE YOUR STARTUP

Asset-Based Valuation

An asset-based business valuation will total up all the investments in the company; this can be done by using the book value of the business (this is a deduction of the liabilities from the assets) or by determining the liquidation value (the net cash that will be left after all assets are sold and debts and liabilities are paid off in the event of a winding up).

The word "asset" includes both tangible and intangible assets of the business. In essence, the intellectual property materials, technology, etc. form part of the assets of a company. All of the assets are given a fair market value which takes into consideration wear outs and property value on an "as is" basis and not purchase amount.

Intrinsic Valuation

This tends to value the startup solely based on the perception of its true value. This perception is usually based on the startup's financial performance and potentials. Most times, the intrinsic valuation of a business is based on the free cash flow of the business. It is calculated as the net present value of the future cash flow of the business.

The details of this form of valuation is mostly not applicable to early-stage businesses. This is because you are required to project the future cash flows of the business based on its historical performance and future strategy. However, there is rarely a sufficient historical context, justifying the forecast will be extremely difficult. This method is best suited for most mature companies that have gone through various stages of funding.

Relative Valuation

This is an attempt to value the business based on the valuation of a comparable business. This is less technical and much more applicable to most startups. If you want to value Uber, for example, relative valuation suggests that the valuation multiple of Uber will be similar to that of Lyft or other cab businesses operating in Nigeria with a similar model.

In identifying the comparable company, you need to find businesses operating in similar markets. This may prove to be difficult because two companies may be in the same industry but have different valuation and most private companies do not disclose their valuation information.

To therefore get the best from the relative valuation approach, you have to seek emerging markets, then find businesses that are at a similar stage as your startup. You will be comparing apples with mangoes if you compare the valuation multiple of a brand at peak level with a brand at startup level; the markets are different, so also are the stages of the businesses and the quality of their team, hence the difficulty.

It is largely difficult to find a perfect comparable in Nigerian market. Where you are condemned to a semi-perfect comparable, some adjustments can be made to reflect the stage or the market of the Target startup. It is also best practice to use more than 3 comparable companies as this will give a much more robust valuation picture and increase the accuracy of the valuation.

UNDERSTANDING TERM SHEETS

A term sheet is a document that outlines the terms by which an investor (angel or venture capital investors) will make a financial investment in your company. It is a bulleted list, prepared by any of the parties, enumerating some of the features as well as the terms and conditions of a contemplated business agreement. The terms and conditions contained in the document are not typically binding on any of the parties, as they are subject to modification through further negotiations before the final agreement is prepared and signed.

A term sheet is an important document because it contains a list of indicative terms and conditions, reflects the intention of the parties entering into a funding or financing arrangement and establishes relationships between investors, venture capital providers, start-ups, and other firms. Ultimately, it reduces the time required to negotiate a business agreement.

KEY CONCEPTS OF THE TERM SHEET

In general, there are two major themes underlying the terms that venture capitalists vigorously negotiate in term sheets; they are:

1. Economic Terms.
2. Control Terms

Economic Terms

This relates to the returns the investors will ultimately get in the event of liquidation; this could either be as a result of the sale of such company or an Initial Public Offering (IPO) and the terms that have a direct impact on this return.

The terms that make up the economics of the deal include:

- Price
- Liquidation preference.
- Pay-to-play.
- Vesting.
- The employee pool.
- Anti-Dilution.

A.   PRICE

The price of the deal is the major focus for the entrepreneur as this ultimately determines the monetary value that would be gotten from the VC deal. While the price per share is the ultimate measure of what is being paid for the equity being bought, price is often referred to as valuation.

There are two ways to value the company, there is the pre-money valuation which is what the investor is valuing the company as at the moment, before investment, and the post-money valuation is the valuation of the company after the investment (i.e. pre-money valuation plus the investment amount).

The next part of the price to focus on is the phrase 'fully diluted.' Both the company and the investor will want to make sure the company has sufficient equity (or stock options) reserved to compensate and motivate its workforce. This is also known as the employee pool or option pool.

Although a large option pool will make it less likely that the company will run out of available options, the size of the pool is taken into account in the valuation of the company, thereby effectively lowering the actual pre-money valuation.

The price implications and factors can be put in simple formulas:

1. Pre-money valuation = Valuation of the startup today, as at the time of the price offer.

2. Post money valuation = Pre-money valuation + Money to be raised by startup.

3. Price per share = Pre-money valuation / existing number of outstanding shares.

4. VC stake = Investment amount Post - money valuation

B. OPTION POOL

The employee pool or option pool is the equity (or stock options) reserved to compensate and motivate the employees of the company workforce. The size of the pool is taken into account in the valuation of the company, thereby effectively lowering the actual pre-money valuation. The typical option pool ranges between 10% and 20%.

C. LIQUIDATION PREFERENCE

The liquidation preference is the next most important economic term after price and impacts how the proceeds are shared in a liquidity event. It is usually defined as a sale of the company or the majority of the company's assets. The liquidation preference is especially important in cases where a company is sold for less than the amount of capital invested.

To be accurate, the term 'liquidation preference' should pertain only to money returned to a particular series of the company's stock ahead of other series of stock. There are two components that make up what most people call the liquidation preference: the actual preference and participation.

I. The actual preference means that a certain value or multiple of the original investment per share is returned to the investor before the common shares receive any consideration. Usually, it is the amount of money invested.

II. Participation is the right of the investor's shares to participate. There are three varieties of participation – Full, Capped and No participation.

D. THE PAY-TO-PLAY PROVISION

This requires that the investor must keep investing at a prorated rate in future financings to not have their preferred stock converted to common stock when there is a bigger investor. It is good for a company and it lets the investors agree to support the company during its life cycle; if not, they have their shares converted to common shares and lose all rights associated with preferred stock.

E. THE VESTING PROVISIONS

Stock and options of founders and key employee's vests over a period (typically, four years). This means that where such employees leave the company before the end of the vesting period, the vesting formula applies and only a percentage of the stock is given.

F. THE ANTI DILUTION PROVISIONS

This is used to protect the investors if shares are to be sold for a lower value than in previous financing rounds.

Control Terms

Control refers to the mechanisms that allow the investors either to affirmatively exercise control over the business or to veto certain decisions the company can make.

If you are negotiating a deal and investors are digging their heels in on a provision that does not impact the economics or control, they are often blowing smoke, rather than elucidating substance.

There are a variety of control terms that effectively give them control of many activities of the company.

A. THE BOARD OF DIRECTORS

There should always be a proper balance among the investor, company, the founder and outside representation in the composition of the board. In the case of a mature company, there will typically be more board members with more outside board members consisting of experienced entrepreneurs and executives.

B. THE PROTECTIVE PROVISIONS

These are the veto rights that investors have on certain actions by the company. Typically, it means that the company cannot agree to do certain things unless the investor agrees. Examples include:

i.   Change the terms of stock owned by the investor.
ii.   Authorise the creation of more stock.
iii. Issue stocks that rank above or are similar to those of the investors.
iv.   Sell the company.
v.   Change the certificate of incorporation details or articles of association of the company.
vi.   Borrow money.
vii. Pay or declare a dividend.

The above-named rights are protective provisions, they do not eliminate the ability to do these things, but simply require the consent of the investors.

C. THE DRAG-ALONG RIGHT

This gives a subset of the investors the ability to force, or drag along, all of the other investors and the founder to carry out a sale of the company. The most common practice is to grant this right to the majority of the stockholders both common and preferred.

D. THE CONVERSION

The Preferred shareholders have the right at any given time to convert their stock into common stock. This allows the buyers of preferred stock to convert to common stock, should they determine on a liquidation event that they would be better off getting paid on an 'as-converted to common' basis rather than on preference and the participation amount.

There are other terms that may feature in a term sheet. They include subjects relating to dividend, redemption rights, information rights, voting rights, restriction on sales, right of first refusal, tag-along rights, etc. Considering the intricacies of the subject matter, we recommend that you consult a business advisory law firm to guide your conversation.

CHAPTER FOUR

FINANCING YOUR BUSINESS

INTRODUCTION

Business organisations and entrepreneurs would usually require startup capital and adequate funds to finance their operations upon starting business. This usually leaves them with a series of financing options. Deciding on the appropriate financing option is an important one that has a major impact on the success or otherwise of your business organisation. This is why it is best to decide early on the financing option that is best suited to the reality of your business at every stage of its growth.

The various innovative forms of financing that you as a business owner could employ to raise capital range from informal forms like self-financing also known as bootstrapping to other forms of borrowing like lending from friends and family members to more structured informal financing options like crowdfunding.

Let us take the example of an entrepreneur; Debbie, who needs money to set up a new business that would deal in handling outsourced duties from various corporate bodies. She decides to explore the options available to her so she can get funds to invest in her business so that she can purchase laptops, get a space and meet other financing needs.

Debbie can reach out to friends and family or use her personal finances and savings (this counts as informal borrowing). After making the choice of reaching out, she was lucky and found family and friends that were willing to invest in her business.

Her business started growing and she needed to increase her staff strength, get a bigger space and more equipment. Debbie would need more structured and formal ways of raising capital and you may also be in the same shoes as Debbie.

This chapter focuses on debt and equity capital. It also addresses the concept of bootstrapping and informal lending.

BOOTSTRAPPING

Let us go back to our example of Debbie.

Debbie has been nursing the great business idea and it has been consuming all her thoughts. So, she smashes her piggy banks, gets money from her savings accounts, withdraws the return on investments she has, counts all these funds into an accumulated sum.

She has so much hope in this business idea that she also goes on to quit her 9 to 5 job as a banker and uses the little capital she has to birth this idea.

The effect of personally financing the business idea means that she has to cut down on luxuries, get her product and services in the market and subsequently build a customer base.

What has happened in this scenario is that Debbie just bootstrapped her business.

What is Bootstrapping?

Bootstrapping is the self-funding of a business by an entrepreneur from personal funds, personal finances and revenue that has been generated from other business activities with no additional funding from external sources. Some entrepreneurs bootstrap throughout the lifetime of their business while others bootstrap only during the early stages before getting external funding.

Bootstrappers will usually employ this option while relying on personal income, savings over time, sweat equity, activities with the lowest possible operating costs, sale of products with fast inventory turnaround and an immediate cash-only approach to selling.

Why Do Entrepreneurs Bootstrap?

There are few funding options in Nigeria. Many entrepreneurs are therefore usually left with limited choices. It is possible that these funding options exist but there is the tendency that fresh entrepreneurs may not be able to raise funds because of certain constraints like a proven profit-making record, proving demand for commodities (products or services) and feasible future plans for profitability.

Bootstrapping can be done for at least one of the following reasons;

- When there is no alternative; or
- To retain control and independence

Bootstrapping is most suitable for business models designed to generate cash from the first day or businesses that need little or no cash to establish. Not all businesses can be easily bootstrapped. A majority of successful bootstrapped companies have a business model that supports an almost instantaneous cash return on invested funds. Without an immediate cash inflow on products, you can burn out your reserved funds (savings) before getting the required demand for your products or services. There is basically no time to test the waters and try to build your customer base first.

Bootstrapping works more often than not but it may not support all business types, for example, some capital-intensive businesses like manufacturing and construction are more difficult to bootstrap because of the amount of funds required to start them up, an entrepreneur that plans to delve into this forms of business will need to purchase heavy machinery and equipment.

Bootstrapping allows you to keep control and ownership of your company and you eventually end up keeping your trade secrets in the long run since you are not going to be involved in trying to convince investors to invest and then have to say too much to the investors about the business. If you are successful at bootstrapping and you later decide to lure investors, your business valuation would have increased and you can get more funds for less equity at that point from investors.

Bootstrapping may be a good option when your industry has little or no pressure, but where your product is competitive and there are a number of giants within the industry, you may need to move faster and bootstrapping may therefore not be your best option.

If you decide to bootstrap your business, make sure you keep records of every penny that is invested in the business. Where you cut down on your periodic allowances, take stock of the difference between your ideal allowances and the paid allowances.

These records will help you to justify your inputs to the business years down the line.

EQUITY CAPITAL

D ebbie's business has grown over the years and the next big step is a wide expansion of business activities which would require funds and finances beyond Debbie's personal financing power. This means that more formal modes of financing her business will be employed like issuing equity or getting a loan (debt).

Equity capital financing is the process of raising capital through the sale of company shares. Equity capital represents some form of investment which confers on a person, ownership stake in a company. If you seek to lure investors to purchase company shares, you should invest in understanding your company valuation as that is one of the factors used to decide the per unit value of company shares.

If you intend to sell your company's shares to raise money, it is better not to allocate the whole of the company shares at the point of registering with the Corporate Affairs Commission.

In terms of tax efficiency, allocation of shares to raise funds is quite a friendly option as there are no taxes in Nigeria on the allocation of shares. The Capital Gains Tax Act exempts any gains realised by a person from a disposal of shares from capital gains tax.

In addition, the Stamp Duties Act also exempts instruments for the transfer of shares (i.e. share transfer agreements) from the payment of stamp duty.

Types of Equity

Equity investors are entitled to ownership rights in the company they invest in. If you want to bring investors into your business, you may issue at least two different types of equity. The two main types are ordinary shares (otherwise known as common shares) and preferred shares.

What is a common share?

A common share is also known as "ordinary shares". It represents an ownership interest in a company that comes with voting rights and cash flow rights (otherwise known as an entitlement to dividends). The Board of Directors of every company usually meet to decide the portion of company profit that should be declared as dividends every year; those dividends are paid to shareholders and the rights to such distribution is what is otherwise known as the shareholders' cash flow rights.

What is a preferred share?

Companies also have the option of issuing preferred shares. As the name implies, they are shares that give preference to their holders. For instance, when a company issues dividend, preference shareholders receive dividends before common shareholders. They also rank higher on the priority claims list; if a company ceases operations, they are settled before common shareholders. Preference shares are usually redeemable; they can or may be bought back by the company at a future date. In fact, the Nigerian law provides that any redeemable share of the company will be regarded as a preference share.

Under the Nigerian law, you cannot by a company's articles of association authorise or issue shares that have more than one vote per share or issue non-voting shares. Preference shares are however exempted from the rule of "one vote per share".

Although there are other forms of equity capital securities like convertible bonds and warrants, the options available to a company raising money from equity financing are more limited than those available for debt financing as the company only has the more prevalent option of issuing shares.

Equity investment usually creates a more inclusive commitment because the investors are involved in the operations, decision making and organisation of the company, as the investor becomes one of the owners of the company as a result of the equity held.

Convertible Shares (Convertible Bonds)

A convertible bond is a hybrid security. A hybrid security is one that has features of both equity securities and debt securities. A convertible bond usually starts off as a debt security with the option to convert it into an equity security.

A convertible bond is a security instrument issued by a company that gives the bondholder the right to convert the bond into common shares of the company.

The number of redeemable common shares is usually agreed on at the point of obtaining the debt security. The option to convert must be exercised before the maturity date of the debt failure of which may make the option expire.

BROAD CATEGORIES OF EQUITY FINANCING

When a company receives finance in exchange for ownership stake in the company, it is most times referred to as equity finance. The financier is also known as an "equity investor". As an equity investor, you partake in the entrepreneurial risk of the business and your returns on investment is entirely dependent on the success of the company.

The main categories of equity finance are–

Private equity; and
public equity.

Public equity usually involves shares of public companies. They are characterised by the fact that invitation can be made through public media to members of the public to invest in them. Public equity is also capable of being traded on the floor of the Nigeria Stock Exchange. A company has to be listed on the floor of the Nigeria Stock Exchange to sell its shares there.

In contrast, private equity involves companies that are traded privately through private placement. A private placement happens when a company makes a private offer to specific individuals to invest in its shares. While public equity investors are not generally involved in the management of the company, private equity financiers provide advice and assist the founders or managers in the development of the business.

We will be focusing more on private equities.

PRIVATE EQUITY

Private equity financing could happen in a lot of ways. In most cases, the enterprise obtains funds from private sources and gives ownership stake in exchange. The private sources may include wealthy individuals, investment funds or institutions, angel investors, venture capitalists, etc. Their capital is made available to the business with assurances of participation in profit sharing through dividends.

Compared to other forms of external finance, the investor accepts more risk and expects returns as far as the business is in existence and continues to do well. Most private equities may not be qualified to be traded in any public stock market.

Private equity is ideal across the entire life cycle of a business. It could feature as seed finance, growth capital or even buyouts (where shares are bought from existing shareholders and control of the company is acquired).

The major actors in private equity are venture capitalists and angel investors. Venture capitalists (VCs) are usually professional investors that specialise in using other people's funds to invest in businesses. They are most times corporate entities and their funding could be targeted at supporting the various stages of development of a business.

Although venture funds are assumed to be the main source of seed and early stage financing, the majority of venture capitalists intervene at a later stage when the worthiness and proficiency of an organisation can be determined and predicted so that they can finance full-scale marketing and production.

Conversely, angel investors are usually individual investors who invest their personal money as private equity. They mostly invest at the seed and early stage of a company and they are often referred to as "informal investors".

FEATURES OF EQUITY CAPITAL

1.   Equity capital vests ownership interests in the investors.
2.   Equity capital dilutes the ownership and control of the

company because it involves giving voting rights to investors. If you are a founder seeking equity investment, one of the things to prepare for is share dilution which sometimes results in loss of control of the company.

3. Equity investors bear the same risks as the founders of the company and as such, are more interested in the success of the company and committed to offering valuable advice and assistance to ensure that the company grows.

4 The arrangement does not permit the investor to reclaim investment sum, rather it permits the investor to be entitled to dividends.

5. In the priority of claims in a winding up process, equity investors (especially ordinary shareholders) are last on the list and they would be paid after all debts owed by the company to lenders and other liabilities have been settled.

6. The company has no obligation to repay equity capital since it is not a direct borrowing.

7. Equity capital does not require any form of collateral to raise capital. What it requires is the ability of the board to sell the company's vision convincingly to would-be investors.

Advantages of Equity Capital

Although many may see giving other people a stake in their business as losing control, this does not have to be the case. Experienced investors can give expert advice to you as an entrepreneur and they can also be helpful in running the business and establishing useful business connections. Another advantage of equity investment is the flexibility and how parties can be creative with the terms that guide them. One big advantage of selling equity stakes to investors is that if your business loses money or gets broke, you likely would not have to pay investors a dime.

Disadvantages of Equity Capital

The biggest disadvantage of equity capital is the loss of control in your business. There are many instances where the founders of a business get voted out after putting in a lot of time, effort and resources. When you think of raising funds by giving out equity, be sure that the financing gain outweighs the effects of the loss of control in the business. The other main disadvantage is that equity investors will want to receive a portion of the profits, this occasions in lower revenue available to reinvest in the business. Finally, because equity investors are now co-owners, you have a duty to inform them of all significant business events. In fact, the law protects their right to attend the general meetings of the company and you cannot by private arrangement exclude their voting rights. They can therefore sue you if they feel their rights are being infringed upon.

DEBT CAPITAL

Debt capital is capital acquired by borrowing funds to be repaid at the expiration of a specified period, usually with interest. It is also sometimes referred to as a borrowed capital usually with some form of interest. The term 'borrowing' is used to mean either borrowing by way of a loan (usually from a bank or other financial institutions) or by way of issuing debt securities such as notes, bonds or commercial paper.

Unlike an equity investor who takes on more risk when purchasing a company's equity with usually no guarantee of returns on the investment, debt investors typically have less risk due to the predetermined tenor, repayment period and interest rates which are contractually binding on parties. On the face of it, debt is a lot cheaper than equity because what your company will pay back (principal sum and interest) is predictable and the company's board can set its mind on it.

Where issue may arise is when the company is unable to repay in which case it may be exposed to the risk of court action and in the extreme case be forced to wind up. When your company makes the decision to procure a loan, you might want to make it convertible to equity so that if the company is unable to repay at the appropriate time, the debt can be valued and converted to equity at an agreed price per share so as to save the company from accruing interest which may lead to the liquidation of the business.

Very few companies have enough cash from equity capital or retained profits to meet every financial obligation as they become due, therefore the option to borrow funds from financial institutions and other lenders is sometimes inevitable. A company may have expectations of future profits or income but requires money upfront to meet its immediate obligations. Where these obligations are urgent and short-term, equity capital might be unsuitable. As noted earlier, debt might be by way of a loan or by way of debt security.

Bank lending is the most common source of external finance for many SMEs and entrepreneurs, which are often heavily reliant on traditional debt to fulfill their start-up, cash flow and investment needs. Banks are the single largest financier of businesses and every entrepreneur must invest time to understand banks' operation, their packages and the regulatory framework for their lending.

If you are an early stage business and you need finance, it may be helpful to avoid short term finances because business may sometimes be equated with a seed that needs time to grow.

The pressure of trying to meet up with repaying short-term financing can stunt the growth of a business and even end the life of the business.

Notwithstanding government policies that mandate banks to devote a portion of their deposits to microlending, fast growing companies with a high risk-return profile may find it hard to access loans on flexible and realistic repayment terms, such companies may therefore need to leverage on other forms of financing.

Below are some of the questions that bank would like to ask if you are seeking for loan:

1. What will the loan be used for?
2. Are there other sources of financing to help spread the risk?

3. How much is needed?
4. When will the money be repaid?
5. When is the money needed?
6. Is it needed in full or in batches?
7. How credit worthy Is the borrower?
8. How viable is the business?
9. Is there collateral for the loan?
10. Is there a guarantor? etc.

Some other forms of debt capital are summarily explained below:

Bonds

Corporate bonds are debt obligations issued by private and public entities. By issuing bonds, the company makes a legal commitment to any interest on the principal, independent of the company's performance and to return the principal when the bond matures.

Crowdfunding

Crowdfunding is a technique to raise external finance from a large audience. The distinctive feature of crowd funding is in the fact that funds are pulled together from a large number of people who may in some cases be unrelated.

Broad Categories of Debt

Generally, debt may be issued in the form of secured or unsecured debt.

·Secured debt is when a borrower pledges certain rights to a lender such as property or equipment to secure the loan against default risk.

·Unsecured debt is not backed by collateral, this usually warrants that they pay higher interest rates to compensate for the risk.

Company debts may be secured or unsecured. The security could be floating or fixed charges. When a company's debt is secured on a fixed charge, it means that certain assets of the company have been identified as collateral for the debt. While, floating charge simply means that the loan is not attached to any asset and may therefore be enforced on any asset of the company. The process of attaching a floating charge on specific assets of the company is known as "crystallisation".

FEATURES OF DEBT CAPITAL

· Debt capital is raised by borrowing funds from investors with the undertaking of repayment. Investors in debt capital are known as lenders, creditors or debt holders.

· Debt capital does not dilute the ownership interest and control of the company because the lender does not have a claim to equity in the business.

· The risks of debt capital investors are limited to the loan/debt granted to the company as the relationship between the lenders and the company is restricted to the terms of the debt financing.

· Debt capital investors rank at the top of the priority of claims list in the event a company is to be wound up.

· There is a standing obligation to repay the loan whether or not a company makes a profit, unlike equity investment that is dependent on the declaration and distribution of a profit.

· Lenders usually require collateral or a personal guarantee prior to granting a loan. Consequently, smaller businesses and other companies with insufficient collateral may be unable to access loans from financial institutions. In addition, the lender would usually impose covenants designed to protect the investment.

Advantages of Debt Capital

The biggest advantage of choosing loans is that you maintain control over your business. Unlike equity investors, lenders have no say in your business and are not entitled to your business profits. The only obligation you owe to your lender is to repay the loan as agreed upon. Finally, an advantage that can be very helpful is that loan payments that go towards paying off the interest on the loan can be deducted as a business expense for tax purposes.

Disadvantages of Debt Capital

The biggest disadvantage of loans is that you have to pay back a steady amount on a consistent schedule, and, as anyone who runs a business knows, profits can be anything but steady. You may have to make a large loan payment precisely when you need the cash for your business the most.

Another disadvantage is that many small business owners have to use personal property as collateral to secure the loan, which puts them personally at risk if the business goes bad. Finally, if you are unable to pay the loan back, you may be personally sued by the bank, regardless of whether the loan is secured or unsecured.

CONCLUSION

For a smaller business that might not be in a position to issue debt instruments or access traditional loans from financial institutions, equity capital may be sourced from angel investors and venture capitalists under defined terms. Angel investors and venture capitalists become partial owners of the business and get involved in the growth of the business. Without doubt, both financing options require a good track record, sound business plan, forecasts and financials which provide some comfort to the potential investors.

If you are in the formation stage of your business, it makes sense to strongly consider selling an equity stake in your business in order to secure financing to get it off the ground. Equity sales are advantageous because they do not require any repayment, and most businesses don't turn a profit for a significant time period, which makes paying back loans extremely difficult.

If you are an established business and have ongoing financing needs, then loans may make a lot more sense. Loans are easier to deal with when a company has enough cash flow to make repayment realistic, and an established company likely has more collateral to offer to secure the loans. Finally, it's worth noting that loans and equity are treated differently for tax purposes, so consult with a business tax advisor to see if one course of action makes more sense than the other.

It is possible to have a mixture of both options. Always seek advice from a professional before opting for any form of capital.

CHAPTER FIVE

DEFINING RELATIONSHIPS THROUGH CONTRACTS

WHY DO YOU NEED PRE-INCORPORATION CONTRACTS?

As a startup founder, you need to protect your company by ensuring that you cover various legal bases and this may require signing contracts even before the company is registered.

Usually, registration confers legal personality on a company (except if the company is registered as a business name or a limited partnership). What this means is that before registration, a company does not have any legal existence and generally if any agreement is done in the name of the company before the registration; the agreement would be invalid.

The legal implication of having a separate legal personality is that when a company is registered, it can sue and be sued in its own name as it is considered an artificial person.

Before you register a company, there may be a need to execute contracts on behalf of the company with the intention to have the contracts binding on the company upon its registration. Before registration, a company does not exist and it cannot validly do anything (like enter into contracts, purchase a property in its name, etc.). No one can therefore in the ordinary sense act as the company's agent or perform any acts on behalf of the company. This is because an agent cannot act for a non-existent principal.

However, there is sometimes the need to start a contract on behalf of a company that is yet to be registered. It is for that reason that certain contracts are permissible at the pre-incorporation stage. A person or a group of persons who are usually promoters may sign these contracts on behalf of the soon to be registered company. These contracts are referred to as pre-Incorporation contracts.

Such a contract may be ratified by the company after its registration. By ratification, we mean that the terms and conditions contained in the contract are, upon registration, approved by the company as binding on it as if originally signed by it.

Upon ratification, the company becomes bound by the contract and is entitled to the benefits as if the company had been in existence at the date of the contract and had been a party to the contract. The company becomes bound and is entitled to the benefits and obligations under the contract.

Prior to the ratification of the contract, or where the contract is not ratified, the person or persons who purported to act on behalf of the company are personally bound by the contract and are entitled to the benefit and liability of it, unless there is an express agreement to the contrary.

THE ESSENTIAL PRE-INCORPORATION CONTRACTS FOR BUSINESSES

There are quite a number of essential contracts that you may want to enter into on behalf of your business before registration depending on your business' industry or sector. Below are some of the major ones that may be essential to virtually every business owner.

- Founders' Agreement
- Shareholders' Agreement
- Intellectual Property Assignment Agreement
- Memorandum and Articles of Incorporation
- Memorandum of Understanding
- Non-Disclosure Agreements
- Regulatory permits and other steps which may be preconditions for the incorporation of a company.

Founders' Agreement

A founders' agreement will be necessary where there are two or more founders in a startup. As a startup founder, you will have the need to create agreements that will regulate your relationship with the other founder(s) if any.

Founders' Agreements are also referred to as Operating Agreements. Founders' agreements serve as operating agreements and are usually created to cover issues like ownership, responsibility, decision-making and other necessary details to be determined between the founders. In case of startups with multiple founders or founding parties, it becomes necessary for them to sign an agreement that defines the working relationship of all parties and manage any conflicts that may arise in the future.

To avoid any dispute among the founding partners of a startup and to ease the resolution of disputes if they arise, all co-founders should sign a comprehensive founders' agreement. Next, we will look at what your founders' agreement should contain.

What Should Your Founders' Agreement Contain?

Some of the fundamental terms that every founders' agreement should contain are:

Roles and Responsibilities: It is important that the roles and responsibilities of the founders are clearly defined. This would help you effectively run your startup. A major mistake made by many startup founders is that they expect every decision to be made collectively by all the founders.

This does not mean that all the founders should not be carried along with the decision making and operations of the startup, however, there is a need to clearly map out distinct responsibilities to avoid conflict.

Equity Holding: The amount of equity held by each Founder and any condition as to vesting if applicable. "Vesting clause" usually helps founders to maintain commitment to the business across the infant period of the business and to also justify the stake of each of the founders during investment rounds.

Dispute Resolution Clause: This usually prescribes how conflicts which may arise with the founders will be resolved. The best practice is usually for parties to consider direct negotiation, or third-party mediation, and then arbitration.

It may help founders to as much as possible keep conflicts away from courts for the fact that it is a public channel of resolving disputes and privacy is not guaranteed.

Shareholders Agreement

This agreement usually contains the rights of shareholders and defines when and the instances in which they can exercise those rights.

Shareholders agreement can either be Equity Shareholders Agreement or Service Shareholders Agreement.

An Equity Shareholders Agreement regulates the ownership rights of shareholders who purchased or promised to purchase interest in the company through considerations which may be monetary, assets, etc.

A Service Shareholder Agreement is applicable where the shareholder's stake is as a result of services to be rendered to the company over a period of time. In this kind of arrangement, it is important to agree on a vesting period for shares, job description of service shareholder, reasonable metrics for ascertaining that the service shareholder meets company's target across timelines, etc.

What Should Your Shareholders Agreement Contain?

- The details of parties to the Agreement (The Shareholders)

- Share Subscription

- Shareholders' right to transfer shares and restrictions of transfer of shares if any:

- Right of first refusal/Preemptive rights.

- Redemption upon the death of the shareholder.

- Organisation and management of the company: the board of directors, the composition of the board, obligations of the directors, removal and replacement of nominees, etc.

- Dividend policy.

- Dispute resolution.

- Choice of legal jurisdiction.

The above-listed terms are generic terms. However, the agreement can contain these terms and some other details which may be specific to the particular arrangement.

Memorandum of Understanding (MOU)

A Memorandum of Understanding is usually entered into by parties before the main transaction itself is done. MOUs sometimes perform the function of a forerunner to agreements that are intended for thereafter. They help the parties involved to reach a mutual understanding about the arrangement they intend to have. Being that MOUs are forerunners to Agreements, they most times are not enforceable except it is obvious from the content that parties intended it to be enforceable.

What Should Your Memorandum of Understanding contain?

- It should describe the parties
- The purpose of the Memorandum of Understanding
- The intended transaction
- The obligations of the parties
- The role and responsibilities of the parties.
- Specific terms and conditions for the purpose of the intended transaction

Non-Disclosure Agreements (NDA)

As a startup founder, it is very important that you sign Non-Disclosure Agreements. An NDA is a contract entered into for the purpose of protecting the confidentiality of information between the parties to the agreement. NDAs could be entered into with prospective employees, investors, service providers, consultants, etc. NDAs protect third party access to the information that is shared between parties. NDAs protect your business by safeguarding your intellectual property and highly sensitive information.

NDAs could be mutual or one-sided. Mutual NDAs are for

when two or more parties are disclosing information and one-sided is for when it is one party that intends to disclose confidential information to the other party.

What should your NDAs contain?

- What constitutes confidential information.

- Who owns the confidential information?

- How confidential information should be handled. This is usually done by including a non-circumvention clause which restricts the use of the confidential information shared for any other purpose other than the transaction agreed on by the parties.

- The period of time within which the confidentiality should be maintained.

- Non-circumvention clause which restricts the use of the information shared.

- Choice of legal jurisdiction.

Intellectual Property (IP) Assignment Agreement

Startups are mostly built on intangible property; we will discuss this better in chapter six. The best practice is usually to assign all intellectual property to the company.

When you start building your company, there may be different individuals helping out. These individuals could be your co-founders, contractors or your team members. An IP assignment agreement ensures that the work they do for your company belongs to your company. This is usually used to assign to the company any intellectual property before the company is formed. By this, all intellectual property rights used to build the startup are assigned to the company.

Intellectual property assignment agreements are different from technology assignment agreements. Technology Assignment Agreements are usually signed by the founders and others engaged to work on the startups especially developers. An example is contracting a freelancer to build an application for your company.

Invention Assignment Agreement

This is usually used after the formation of the company. The company by this agreement is assigned any right that may arise for relevant products created by employees in the ordinary course of business of the employee after the company is formed.

By this agreement, the company owns rights to the IP portfolio and it is assigned to the company. As an alternative to this Agreement, the Founders may insert an intellectual property ownership clause in the Employment Agreement to be handed to employees.

Memorandum and Articles of Incorporation

The Articles of Association is a document that defines the company's internal constitution while the company's Memorandum of Association regulates the company's external affairs. It also states the amount of share capital the company has and how it is divided among the shareholders.

These documents are to be filed alongside the other forms required in the process of registering the company. They are contracts between the company and its shareholders. It goes on to set out the rights and duties of the shareholders and regulates the activities of the Board of Directors.

CONCLUSION

Pre-Incorporation contracts exist because it would be a matter of inconvenience if no official business operation can be performed in the name of the organisation before its registration.

There may be a need to make arrangements for the office, place of work, worker, etc. To ease these inconveniences, the promoters can enter into the agreements for the benefit of the prospective company.

The above listed documents are not exhaustive as there may be a need to create other types of pre incorporation contracts not listed above which may be specific to the startup due to the industry it operates in.

CHAPTER SIX

PROTECTING YOUR COMPANY'S INTELLECTUAL PROPERTIES

The world's familiar properties are visible. They can be touched, felt and physically possessed. However, certain ownerships are locked in materials that originate from intangible objects conceived by the mind and processed through the brain. These works are in their crude form mere ideas' that can only be protected after they are expressed in a finished form.

Let us take an example of a song in a musician's mind, in its crude form as an idea or thought, it cannot be protected until it is expressed in another form by writing the lyrics, meeting with a producer then creating a song from the idea. These classes of works are known as "intellectual properties".

While this series will focus on helping you understand the different intellectual property rights under the Nigerian laws, it may be important to mention quickly that the notion that ideas are not capable of being protected is one that should be reviewed considering the dynamics of technological interventions. With the emergence of the internet and social media, the concept of an idea ought to be considered more closely than before. For example, if an idea is shared via email, will it be said to be an idea or not?

There are different forms of intellectual property rights. They are:

- Copyright
- Patents
- Trademarks
- Industrial Designs
- Trade Secrets

COPYRIGHT

C opyright is the right of an author of a creative work to prevent others from using that work, including copying it. Copyright can cover almost any creative expression (including a book, comic book, writing, or picture). Copyright protection aims to protect information (in whatever form) from being unlawfully copied (repeated) without permission.

You own the copyright to a work by creating the work or otherwise acquiring the copyright to the work from the creator of the work.

Works Protected by Copyright

The following may be protected as copyright under the Nigerian intellectual property laws:

1. Literary works which are mostly expressed thoughts in

writing. Examples of works that fall under this category are books of any kind, films and scripts, computer programs and choreographic works.

2. Musical works.

3. Architectural designs and artistic works like paintings, woodworks, drawings, photographs (excluding moving/motion picture photography which fall under another category; cinematography).

4. Cinematography films (this includes the Master copy of a sequence of visual images otherwise known as moving pictures and the soundtracks recorded alongside)

5. Sound recordings (exempts soundtracks attached to cinematographic film because it is protected under cinematography), and;

6. Broadcasts (these can either be sound or television broadcasts).

Conditions for Protection under Copyright

For a copyrightable work to be protected under the law, it must have fulfilled some conditions:

- The work has to be original; and
- the work must be such that it is capable of being perceived, reproduced or communicated directly or indirectly.

On originality, the work ought to be a result of some substantial and real expenditure of mental and physical energies. The required standards of originality for literary, musical or artistic work is different from works that are a product of cinematograph films, sound recordings or broadcasts; in the case of cinematograph films, sound recordings or broadcasts, if it can be shown that although the work is based on existing work, skills and efforts were deployed to create something original, such work may meet the originality standard and qualify for protection.

For your work to be qualified for protection, you (as the owner) must be a Nigerian citizen or domiciled in Nigeria, otherwise, your work must be such that it was first published in Nigeria. If you are a citizen or a person domiciled in a country with a bilateral agreement with Nigeria, you may be able to claim copyright over your works on certain limited grounds.

The same principle applies to incorporated companies. Your

company must either be registered in Nigeria under Nigerian laws or is registered in or domiciled in a country with a bilateral agreement with Nigeria.

How does Copyright work in an Employer-Employee Relationship?

Some forms of businesses may be such that employees can create works that can be protected by copyright. You need to learn how to protect copyrights that emanate from such relationships.

An employee that creates a copyrightable work in the course of employment has an exclusive right on the work unless the employee is under an agreement with the employer which states otherwise. The exception to relationships that can be protected by an employment relationship is journalism (media companies and newspapers).

Special Records for Press and Production Businesses

If you are a business owner that runs a business as a printing press or deals as a producer, printer or manufacturer of a copyrightable work, the law mandates you to keep a record of works that you do which can be protected by copyright. The records you need to have are:

- Name of author
- Title of work
- Year of production
- Quantity of work produced

Rights of a Copyright Owner

You have an exclusive right to control the carrying out of certain acts in respect of your copyright. The acts include publishing, distribution, translation, broadcasting, recording, reproduction, etc.

As the owner of a copyrighted work, you may sue for breach of the copyright and demand for damages (compensation) for the breach, you can request for an injunction against the further breach of your rights and you may ask that the violator accounts for profit made on your work to determine the extent of the breach. Another option is to initiate steps that would lead to criminal proceedings (and you can do this alongside your civil claims).

If you have a hint of a place where infringing copies, plate, film or any contrivance is being used to illegally produce your work, you can apply to the court to enter the building alongside a police officer to seize the contrivance or even inspect works and other materials in the custody of the suspect.

The lifespan of Copyright

Copyright persists for varying durations depending on the kind of work and ownership. Below is for ease:

Category	Lifespan
Literary, musical or artistic work (except photographs) with authors	70 years after the death of the owner
Literary, musical or artistic work with anonymous authors	70 years after the year of publication
Joint authorship (ownership)	70 years after the death of the author last surviving author
Government or corporate body	70 years after the year of publication
Cinematograph films, photographs and broadcasts	50 years after the year the work was first made

From the descriptions of the lifespan of various kinds of work, it is best practice for authors to own copyrights in their name and capacity and license its use to their companies for the longevity of the lifespan of the work.

What happens after a work expires?

After expiration, there is no provision for renewal. It can be accessed in public space without sanction.

Exceptions to Copyright Protection

The guiding rule of copyright is built on the commandment "thou shall not copy", the rule should be read extensively with the actual position of not commercialising or making profits from another person's work. Thus, if there is little or no substantial copying of your work in a newer one, there is no infringement. In a similar vein, if your work is to be adopted for research, private use, criticism, review, etc. in which your ownership and title are acknowledged, this does not count as an infringement.

A record producer (whether the person recorded or adapted it in Nigeria) will not be said to breach copyright if he/she/it records/adapts a copy of the sound recording for retail sale in Nigeria with the prior consent and license from the owner. To that extent, it is expected that royalties are paid to the owner.

TRADEMARK

B rand valuation expert, David Haigh, points out that "the single largest source of intangible value in a company is its trademark". Trademark is a business' or individual's intellectual property.

We are in a system where people are unable to identify the trademarks in their business and those who can identify it erroneously assume that they are entitled to automatic protection and exclusive right over a trademark the moment they come up with one and continue to use it in their day to day business. This chapter answers questions regarding trademarks, its protection, etc.

Understanding a trademark

The Trade Marks Act of Nigeria defines a mark to mean and include a device, brand, heading, label, ticket, name, signature, word, letter, numeral, or a combination of any of these marks. Trademark is therefore defined according to the Act as a mark used or proposed to be used concerning goods to indicate a connection in the course of trade between the goods and some person having the right either as proprietor or as the registered user to use the mark.

Another definition that is simple and gives a rounded image of a trademark is the definition given by the World Intellectual Property Organisation (WIPO), the organisation defines a trademark as a distinctive sign which identifies certain products or services as those produced or provided by a specific person, enterprise or a group of persons/enterprises allowing the consumer to distinguish them from goods or services of others. It is a sign capable of distinguishing the goods or services of one enterprise from those of other enterprises.

Simply put, a trademark is a unique mark with which a trade or business is identified. It is one unique feature in the mind of your customers that your business is identified with. It is used to differentiate the goods and services of a business from those of another.

Common examples of Trademarks

As mentioned earlier, a trademark includes a name, words, symbols, slogan, numbers, drawings, three-dimensional features, shape, colour or sounds or a combination of these elements.

Examples are;

Brand names: typical examples include Porsche, Toyota, Mercedes Benz, McDonald's, Rolex, Samsung, Apple, Facebook, Nestle, Uber and Netflix

Words: such as Coca-Cola, 7up and a big mac.

Symbols: such as the bitten apple on apple products, the harp symbol on every Guinness product, the Nike swoosh symbols and the Mercedes Benz emblems.

Products shape: such as the Coca-Cola branded bottle shape.

Colours: such as those used by telecommunication companies like MTN (yellow), GLO (light green) and Airtel (Red)

Slogans: such as everywhere you go (MTN), rule your world (GLO).

Sound: the signature Nokia tune.

You can also think of something unique businesses are identified with as the list is endless.

Effect of Registering a Trademark

Your trademark gives a face to your business and enhances your brand in such a way that your customers can easily place a face or distinguish your product or service from those of your competitors or other brands.

While registering your trademark confers an exclusive right to the use of the registered trademark, it also implies that the trademark can be exclusively used by you, or licensed to be used by another person in return for payment.

Registering your trademark gives you the right to approach the Court to prevent, stop or to recover damages for the infringement of your registered trademark.

Registrable Trademarks

The fact that a mark can be protected does not confer an automatic right to registration or protection like copyright. There are conditions a mark must meet for it to be registrable. One major factor that can make a mark unregistrable is generic names. This simply translates to the fact that an acceptable and commonly used name which generally identifies a product cannot be trademarked. Typical examples include shoes, refrigerators, microwaves and other household and everyday appliances with generic names.

For a trademark to be registrable, it must be new, distinctive, not misleading or confusing, not illegal, scandalous or immoral and not similar to existing registered trademarks.

When to Register a Trademark

While there is no timeframe to register your choice mark, it is good practice to register and give your mark protection from illegal use by another before releasing it to the public to ensure that it meets with the standards of newness.

Who Can Register a Trademark?

The body saddled with the responsibility of registering trademarks in Nigeria is the Trademarks, Patents and Designs Registry at the Federal Ministry of Industry, Trade and Investment.

At the registry, only accredited attorneys, agents, individuals or companies can register trademarks on behalf of trademark applicants or owners.

Therefore, you are to appoint an accredited agent to apply for and conclude registration of a choice trademark which is done in four phases which are:

- Availability/Clearance Stage.
- Application filing stage.
- Publication/Advertisement stage.
- Certification stage.

Timeline for completion of registration

An application to register your trademark can be done manually or electronically through the online filing system. The registry provides that registration may be completed within 3-4 months from the date of application but it could be more or less depending on the circumstances of each registration.

Note that where registration is not completed within twelve months from the date of the application because of default on the part of the applicant, the application will be deemed abandoned by the registrar who may give notice of non-completion to the Applicant in writing reminding the Applicant to complete registration within the time specified before taking such decision.

Requirements for registration of a Trademark

While applying to register your trademark, you are to provide your personal or business details where it is to be registered in your name (for business owners) or incorporated company's name, your signature, the class of goods or services to which the mark will apply, a distinctive invented word, a clear picture of the mark including any colours, forms, or three-dimensional features and also pay the necessary fees.

If your company is registered as a business name, it is advisable that the trademark should be registered in your name while it is stated that you are trading in the name and style of your business name (For example, Frank Olawale Bayero trading in the name and style "FOB Company"). This is for the obvious reason that a business name is not a juristic person and cannot own properties in its name.

How to identify a registered trademark.

The fact that a trademark is used by a person does not automatically mean that it is protected under the law. Two symbols can be used to know the status of a trademark and degree of protection. They are ™ and ®.

™ is used for an unregistered mark generally to show that the mark refers to a particular product or service, it is often used by a mark owner to put competitors on notice of the use of a mark and also while the mark is undergoing registration, it can be used for free and without any sanction even where an application to register the mark has not been filed. It, however, does not guarantee protection from unauthorised third party use.

On the other hand, "®" is used for a registered trademark for a product or service to the effect that the mark must only be used by the owner or licensee thereby giving your mark a higher level of protection. In other words, you can only use the ® symbol after your trademark has been duly registered and upon receiving a trademark certificate.

The Lifespan of a Registered Trademark

A trademark once registered is protected for an initial period of seven (7) years in Nigeria and can be renewed for a further period of 14 years from the date of expiration of the original registration or the last renewal of registration, as the case may be from time to time and as long as the mark remains in use. A renewal application should be made not less than three months from the due date of expiry.

Does registration of my trademark in Nigeria give it worldwide protection?

A registered trademark is protected only in the country where it is registered. Registering your trademark in Nigeria only protects it from unauthorised use in Nigeria. To enjoy worldwide protection, you have to register the mark in each foreign country where protection is sought.

While Nigeria is a party to the Paris Convention which provides for the protection of Trademarks in a foreign country and encourages countries to give foreign marks the same protection as local marks, the convention still requires that such mark is registered in each foreign country where the mark is sought to be protected.

Another foreign treaty on the protection of trademark internationally is the 1891 Madrid Agreement which provides for an international trademark registration system which allows your trademark to be protected in several countries by filing a single application called the Madrid system as against multiple registrations in each country. The Madrid system is administered by the World International Property Organisation (WIPO) through the Local WIPO office in the country where the mark originates from (the country where the owner of the mark lives or carries on business).

Once you register a trademark under the Madrid system, it enjoys immediate protection as if the mark has been registered locally in each of the other countries who are parties to the agreement. Nigeria, however, is not yet a party to the treaty. Thus, a Nigerian who desires to have his trademarks protected in a foreign country will have to register it in that country.

PATENTS

A patent is a form of intellectual property that gives its owner the legal right to exclude others from making, using, or selling an invention (a product or process that provides, in general, a new way of doing something, or offers a new technical solution to a problem) for a limited period of years.

It usually refers to the right granted to anyone who invents something new, useful and non-obvious.

Patents are 'duration-specific rights' related to an invention issued in exchange for publicising the invention.

Criteria for Patent Protection

Before a patent can be registered, it has to satisfy certain conditions.

These conditions are highlighted below:

Newness (novelty)

- It must be a product of some inventive activities (a product or process that provides, in general, a new way of doing something, or offers a new technical solution to a problem).

- Capable of industrial application.

- Not exempted (a work must not be contrary to public order, morality, etc.)

Who can register a Patent?

The person that applies to protect a patent has rights to the patent whether or not he/she is the inventor. The patent owner has the exclusive right to prevent or stop others from commercially exploiting the patented invention. Thus, once you register your patent, all exclusive rights belong solely to you.

While as the inventor you have a right to recognition as the creator of the product or process, any person that applies first for the protection of a patent owns all rights to the patent.

Implication of Registration

Does it mean you can steal another person's patent and rush to register?

This cannot be done because the law provides that if you can prove that the essential elements of the registered patent were obtained from your invention, the right to the registered patent will become yours.

Who owns the rights to a patent in an employment relationship?

In employment relationships, the right to a patent rests in the employer. An employee may, however, have a right to fair remuneration depending on the significance of the invention and especially where under job description, there was no duty to engage in the inventive activity.

Similarly, if you engage someone to make an invention on a contractual basis, you have a right to the invention.

Who owns the rights to a patent in an assignor-assignee relationship?

Where an assignor-assignee relationship exists, the assignment must be done by way of a written contract and that contract ought to be registered with the Registrar of Patents. An assignor is someone who by an agreement with the inventor has the right to a patent.

If you intend to license your invention, you may consider limiting the scope of authority (i.e. give a limited scope of the license) or give general authority.

Registration of Patents

The first step to register a patent is to conduct a preliminary check at the patent and design registry to ensure the invention has not already been patented.

The next step is for you to prepare your application. The application should contain the background of the invention, the industry in which the invention is applicable, a summary of how the invention works, diagram description of the invention, details of the inventor and applicant.

If you are acting through an agent, the agent's details would also need to be included. After submitting the application and necessary documents, then you may pay the necessary fees.

Bear in mind that the scope of your rights against the public will be determined by the quality of your application (components like the description and drawings of your invention). It is advisable that all illustrations and descriptions are succinct and detailed.

Effect of a Patent Registration

As the registered owner of a patent, you have the right to exclusively commercialise the patent (i.e. making, importing, selling, etc.) whether it is a process or a product.

Where the patent is a 'Process' and not a 'Product', you have an exclusive right to apply the process for commercial purposes.

As the owner of a registered patent, you may sue for infringement of your patent and demand for damages (compensation), you can request for an injunction against the further breach of your rights, you may ask that the violator accounts for profit made on using your patent.

Another option is to initiate steps that would lead to criminal proceedings (and you can do it alongside your civil claims). If you have a hint of a place where infringing copies, plate, film or any contrivance is being used to illegally produce your work, you can apply to the court to order that the infringing copies of your patent be delivered for destruction.

Is there a danger in registering a patent and not doing anything with it?

What happens when a patent is registered and the inventor is not maximising its use? In such a situation, another person may apply to use the invention in an economically viable way. This option can be exploited in any of the following situations:

If your patent has the capability of working in Nigeria but has not been put to work.

Where there is more need for the invention than you have shown competence to meet.

Where your refusal to grant licence unfairly or substantially hinders the development of industrial activities in Nigeria

Duration of Rights to a Registered Patent

The lifespan of the rights to a registered patent is 20 years from the date of filing which is supposed to be renewed every year. The patent may become invalid if it is not renewed annually, such that you can lose your right to enforce it against the public when there is an infringement.

PROTECTION OF INDUSTRIAL DESIGN IN NIGERIA

Intellectual Property till recently has been considered a luxury that only big companies and enterprises can afford by the industry in general and SMEs in particular. Contrary to this line of thought, it is a major avenue for SMEs and techpreneurs to establish their credentials equally with the large enterprises.

Every business has some valuable intangible property worth protecting. Keeping SMEs abreast of the latest information on Intellectual Property Rights systems and to enable them to protect their IP assets is, indeed, very important at the moment amidst the upsurge of startups and technological advancements. Ignorance in this field may lead to a loss of valuable rights and expensive litigation or both.

WHAT IS AN INDUSTRIAL DESIGN?

An industrial design generally refers to a product's overall form and function, it constitutes the ornamental or aesthetic aspect of an article or object. For businesses, designing a product generally implies developing the product's functional and aesthetic features taking into consideration issues like the product's marketability, the costs of manufacturing or the ease of transport, storage, repair and disposal.

In basic terms, an industrial design is the outward appearance of a product as opposed to the function that the product ought to perform.

The design of an object or product may consist of three-dimensional (3D) features, such as the shape of an article or two-dimensional features, such as patterns, lines or colour. The primary legislation that regulates the intellectual property sector in Nigeria is the Patents and Designs Act. The Nigeria Patents and Designs Act affords protection for two types of designs:

Textile designs – combinations of lines or colours or both.

Product packaging – three-dimensional designs.

The industrial design focuses on aesthetic value and does not protect the technical or functional features of the product, it only applies to the aesthetic nature of a finished product, and it is distinct from any technical or functional aspects.

Besides, it is important to note that Nigeria excludes handicrafts from design protection, as industrial design law in Nigeria requires that the product to which an industrial design is applied is an article of manufacture or that it can be replicated by industrial means.

Handicrafts are bespoke items which are individually made by hand and cannot be made by factory means. (However, industrialisation has brought the advent of various forms of machines some of which can replicate handicraft designs and patterns, this is a grey area which the law should fill soon to avoid technicalities when such products are involved)

USAGE OF INDUSTRIAL DESIGNS IN BUSINESS

Businesses that use industrial designs seek ways to perfect their designs to ensure that it meets all standards set by the primary legislation before they register them. This takes a lot of time and resources (both intellectual, physical and financial).

Designs are created for many reasons, they include:

Designs create awareness about a new product that is attractive to customers and appeals to members of the public.

Create a signature look for products from the line of the design owner that is distinct and identifiable with the design owner.

Alter an existing product to reintroduce it or modify it to morph into a new product line.

By registering a design, you can prevent it from being copied and imitated by competitors and thereby strengthen competitive position.

REQUIREMENTS FOR PROTECTION OF AN INDUSTRIAL DESIGN

1. Newness: A design meets the newness criteria if no identical design has been made available to the public before the date for application for registration. The design owner must not have published the design before seeking to register it.

2. Originality: A design is original if the design owner has independently created it without any form of imitation of a previously existing design. If the design simply makes minor changes to an earlier design, it will not be considered as a new design and as such, it will not be eligible for design protection.

3. The technicality of Function: The design must not be dictated exclusively by the technical function of the product.

4. Protected Emblems: The design must not include protected official symbols or emblems such as the national flag, the coat of arms and other national emblems.

5. Public Order: The design must not be contrary to public order or morality.

HOW TO PROTECT A DESIGN IN NIGERIA

An industrial design must be registered with the Patent and Designs Registry to be protected by the law as peculiar to the design owner. The mode of registration is through an application and when an application is made for the registration of industrial design, the design will be presumed to be new at the time of the application.

The first step to take in registering an industrial design is for you to fill an application form which includes your basic contact details as the applicant. Applications done by an agent appointed by you the applicant require a power of attorney.

After writing the application, you have to file the application at the Patents and Designs registry with the statement of novelty or description attached. The description generally needs to be of the design and not of the product to which it has been applied. It should be accurate and adequate in differentiating it from any similar earlier designs. It should cover all the distinctive aesthetic features of the design and should describe which feature(s) is/are the most important and which the applicant seeks to protect. This is contained in the Design rules and may not be an immediate requirement for registration, but for protection of the design in case a matter is filed in court, this will be one of the necessary documents required to prove registration.

The Registry then issues an acknowledgement notice to you confirming receipt of the application. After the acknowledgement notice is received, the appropriate filing fees are paid.

The design is registered only after undertaking a formal examination to ensure that administrative formalities have been complied with and a substantive examination checking the existing designs on the register for novelty and/or originality and to ensure the design is not contrary to any public order. If the application meets the requirements, acceptance notice is issued and if it is refused, a refusal notice is issued.

Once a design is registered, it is entered into the design register and a design registration certificate is issued.

IMPLICATION OF REGISTRATION OF DESIGN

Drawing up an illustration or pattern of industrial design in Nigeria does not suffice as protection of that design for your usage. Any design or design owner who wants the protection of a design must register the same with the Patents and Designs registry as stated above. The right to the registration of a design is vested in the person who is the first to apply for the registration of the design.

A registered design gives protection to the shape of the product e.g. lines, colours or any three-dimensional form. The idea is to prevent others from reproducing the external design of your product for industrial use. Once you are the owner of a registered design, you can prevent others from reproducing, importing, illicitly profiting, selling or utilising for commercial purposes by reproducing the design.

Let us assume that your company has designed a chair with an innovative design that has eagles flying on the vamp or backrest of the chair, registered it at the Registry of Trademarks, Patents and Designs, and has therefore obtained exclusive rights over chairs bearing that design. What this means is that if you discovered that a competitor is making, selling or importing chairs bearing the same or substantially the same design you will be able to prevent him from using your design and, possibly, obtain compensation for damages which your business has suffered from the unauthorised use of that design. So, while you cannot stop competitors from making competitive products you may prevent them from making products that look just like yours and having a free ride on your creativity.

LIFESPAN OF REGISTERED DESIGN

The registration process of a design typically takes around six months to complete. A registered design is protected for 5 years from the date of the application for registration. Protection may be renewed for two further consecutive periods of 5 years.

PROTECTING YOUR DESIGN FROM UNLAWFUL AND ACCIDENTAL PUBLICATION

If you wish to protect your industrial design, keeping the design confidential is crucial. The reason for this is that the central requirement and key criteria for design protection is generally the novelty of the design, that is, the design must be new. If you are going to show your design to others for some form of assessment or under an employment scenario, it is advisable to have confidentiality clauses in written agreements or non-disclosure agreements, clarifying that the design is confidential.

Failure to keep the confidentiality could affect the validity of a registered design unless it can be proven that the party that publicised it ought to have kept it a secret.

LAWFUL PRIOR PUBLICATION OF DESIGN

There is an exemption under the law that protects prior publication of industrial design. The Law provides that any design that has been published by way of an official exhibition or trade show six months before the application to register the design shall not be held to have been published.

This exemption is sensitive and should be read carefully as a design that has already been disclosed to the public by, for example, advertising the same in your company's catalogue or brochure may no longer be considered new for registration and protection of a design. It becomes part of public knowledge and cannot be protected by the exemption.

Also, a product that is introduced in an official exhibition or trade show must be registered soon enough. If after six months of such exhibition the design has not been registered, it has fallen outside the exemption provided by the law and shall become published at that moment.

HOW INDUSTRIAL DESIGNS AFFECT YOUR BUSINESS

If your business enterprise deals with products that require a design to be drawn up for your products, you should always seek protection for that design to avoid imitation. This is especially sensitive for startups whose ideas can be stolen by the bigger guns and monetised beyond the startups' capabilities. For these businesses, the issue of design should always be integrated into their business strategy.

In general, the person who created the design or, if working under contract, his employer, can apply for registration. Where it is under contract employment, the employer shall be the owner as long as it was created during the regular and normal job description of the employee and where it was outside his duties, it may be transferred by a formal agreement coupled with certain incentives. For example, if an employee designs a new multi-functional water bottle which is not within his daily duties, he can transfer the same to the company if the company will better publicise it and bring in more profit and customers with a percentage cut in an agreement. This also applies to external contractors contracted for creating that design.

As entrepreneurs, there should be clauses in employment agreements, contractor agreements and all such agreements that may relate to or occasion for the creation of an industrial design stating ownership rights to cover every loophole that could come up including original illustrations of designs.

The applicant for an industrial design registration can be either an individual (like a designer) or a legal entity (like a company). In either case, the application may be made directly or through an agent.

LICENSING INDUSTRIAL DESIGNS

Industrial designs are licensed when you, the owner of the design (the licensor) grants permission to another person (the licensee) to use the design for whatever mutually agreed on purposes. In such cases, a licensing contract is generally signed between the two parties specifying the terms and scope of the agreement.

Licensing contracts often include certain limitations like the countries where the licensee may use the design, the time for which the license is granted and the type of products for which it can be used. To license the use of the design in foreign countries you would need to have previously obtained, or at least applied for, industrial design protection in the countries concerned.

Authorising others to use your industrial designs through a licensing contract will enable your business to receive an additional source of revenue and is a common means of exploiting a company's exclusivity and ownership over its registered designs.

Agreements to license industrial designs are often included in broader licensing agreements which cover all aspects of a product (i.e. not just the visual elements). Thus, it could cover for both patents, designs, export, resale, percentage of parties amidst other terms.

CONCLUSION

After registration of a design, the next question that comes up is what do I do if another person infringes on my industrial design. These affairs can be somewhat complicated and the best option to explore is to speak to an IP lawyer immediately such infringement is detected. The design owner has to monitor imitation in the market, once an imitation is detected, do not resort to self-help by defaming or publishing spiteful allegations against the violator.

Nigeria's design law needs to expand its applicability to cover for modern trends like the handicraft sector mentioned earlier and another area is digital designs like computer icons and mobile phone icons which many countries now register as designs. However, every SME and company should always seek to protect their IP rights at all times and under all possible areas of its application. The right conferred by registration of an industrial design is absolute in the sense that there is infringement whether or not there has been deliberate copying.

TRADE SECRETS

Trade secrets are intellectual property rights on confidential information which may be sold or licensed. In general, any confidential business information which provides an enterprise with a competitive edge and is unknown to others may be protected as a trade secret.

Trade secrets could be technical information or commercial information. Technical information would include such information concerning manufacturing processes, source codes, pharmaceutical test data, designs and drawings of computer programs. Commercial information includes distribution methods, list of suppliers and clients, and advertising strategies.

Generally, any information which is not in the public domain and provides a competitive edge may be considered a trade secret. The unauthorised use of such information by persons other than the holder is regarded as an unfair practice and a violation of the trade secret.

A trade secret may also be made up of a combination of different elements, each element may by itself be available to the public, but a combination of these elements may make a new formula or recipe which may give the company or individual a competitive advantage over others. Such may be considered a trade secret.

For example, the ingredients to make a cake are well known by all bakers but if Miss P has a special order of mixing the ingredients and the proportions which make up her P Recipe, this makes the P Recipe a trade secret.

There are some conditions for the information to be considered a trade secret. These conditions vary from country to country, some general international standards exist which are contained in Article 39 of the Agreement on Trade-Related Aspects of Intellectual Property Rights (TRIPS Agreement):

Qualities of a Trade Secret

- The information must be 'secret'. For information to qualify as a secret, it must be such that is not generally known or accessible to the public.
- The information must have commercial value because it is a secret.

- It must have been subject to reasonable steps by the rightful holder of the information to keep it secret (e.g., through confidentiality agreements).

A process for the manufacturing of products which allows a company to produce goods more cost-effectively and a competitive edge over competitors may be regarded as a trade secret.

GLOBALLY POPULAR TRADE SECRETS

Let us look at some examples of globally known trade secrets to better understand the subject.

- The New York Times's Best-Seller List
- Coca-Cola Recipe
- Listerine mouthwash secret formula
- Krispy Kreme Doughnut Recipe
- KFC Recipe

The most popular on this list has to be the Coca-Cola recipe. At the end of the nineteenth century, the Coca-Cola company had to make a choice which was; Patent the recipe for its popular soft drink, which would mean disclosing its ingredients, or brand it a trade secret. Executives of the company chose to keep it a trade secret. There have been stringent security measures put in place to keep this recipe safe. In 2006, it was reported that a Coca-Cola employee and two accomplices tried to sell the Coke recipe to Pepsi, however, Pepsi notified the Coca-Cola company and the leak was averted.

Differences Between Trade Secrets and Patents

More often than not, trade secrets can be mistaken for patents depending on the secret. We will go on to examine some major distinctive features between the two forms of intellectual property.

1. A trade secret can be protected for an unlimited period. What this means is that a trade secret can be protected forever or until someone else legitimately discovers the secret. A patent will expire after twenty years from the date of filing of the patent.

2. Unlike patents, trade secrets are protected without registration as there are no procedural formalities for trade secrets.

3. There are also no registration costs for a trade secret, and they go into effect immediately.

4. Trade secrets also have no compliance requirements for registration.

5. A trade secret owner cannot stop others from using the same technical or commercial information, if they acquired or developed such information independently by themselves through their own Research and Development, reverse engineering or marketing analysis. A patent owner can stop others from using such information even where they come by it as a result of independent research. What this means is that trade secrets do not provide "defensive" protection. For example, if a specific process of producing a particular product has been protected by a trade secret, someone else can obtain a patent on the same invention, if the inventor arrived at that invention independently.

6. While every information or process which passes the trade secret test may be kept as such, not all trade secrets are patentable inventions. Examples are marketing plans and strategies, customers list or client database.

7. A trade secret is more difficult to enforce than a patent is. Unlike other intellectual property rights which are statutorily provided for, trade secrets in Nigeria are not governed by codified statutes but are governed by basic legal principles of contract, tort and equity.

he implication of this is that trade secrets are not by themselves protected by law; the breach of trust/contract is what will be enforceable. For example, a perpetual injunction may be issued to discontinue further disclosure of the trade secret. The owner of the trade secret may also apply to recover damages for the loss incurred.

Protecting a Trade Secret

The first thing is to ensure it is not information in the public domain. The next thing would be to make sure that only a limited number of people know the secret. It is important to make a person who knows understand that it is confidential.

A company with a trade secret should also ensure it signs confidentiality agreements while dealing with third parties to ensure that all parties know that the information is a secret and keep it as such. Where such information is used indiscriminately by a competitor or a third party, such action would be considered a violation of the company's trade secrets.

Trade Secrets and Employment Relations

Generally, Employers usually seek to protect their trade secrets from employees, but the fact remains that there will be the need to put other persons in the know as a company cannot be run by just one individual. The problem with trade secrets is that the more people know it, the more susceptible it is to being revealed to competitors. This, therefore, makes it necessary for employers to put measures in place to protect their trade secrets while it is shared with employees.

Some of these measures include;

1. Non-Disclosure/Confidentiality Agreement: When an employee is made to sign a non-disclosure or confidentiality agreement, an employer may sue for damages and may also stop the unauthorised use of the trade secret where such employee defaults.

2. Non-compete Agreement: A clause like this is usually inserted in agreements to protect the employer when the employee leaves the company. It usually requires that the employee does not work with a competitor for some time after leaving the company.

Chapter SEVEN

MASTERING TAX AND LEGAL COMPLIANCES IN YOUR BUSINESS JOURNEY

INTRODUCTION

Learning to navigate the Nigerian business terrain is a necessity for every startup. Although there are industry specific regulatory compliance needs for certain businesses, others are general and apply to all businesses no matter the industry and size.

One obligation that is peculiar to all businesses is compliance with the provisions of the Companies and Allied Matters Act which is administered by the Corporate Affairs Commission. Tax compliance is another and is administered by the various tax agencies created by law.

This chapter will enlighten you on the fundamental knowledge needed for your business compliance with the Corporate Affairs Commission and tax compliances with different tax authorities.

REGULATORY COMPLIANCES UNDER THE COMPANIES AND ALLIED MATTERS ACT

The Companies and Allied Matters Act is the principal law that regulates the incorporation of companies, limited liability partnerships, limited partnerships, registration of business name together with incorporated trustees of communities, bodies, associations, etc. The obligations expected of your business depends on the kind of registration that you did under the law and the activities that you do per time. These obligations are known as "post Incorporation acts". They are matters which arise after your company is registered.

While some of the matters are clearly stated as obligations which must be done annually so long as your business remains in existence, others are as a result of your company's board decision, the partners or that of the proprietor(s) as the case may be. Registering a business is supposed to be the beginning of your journey, not the end of it. Mastering the instructions and guidelines that you must comply with in the course of your sojourn will therefore help you to remain on the right track and also run a good race.

Some post incorporation compliances that might be applicable to your line of business are:

a. Filing of annual returns
b. Change of company name
c. Removal or addition of director
d. Removal or addition of partner
e. Increase or reduction in share capital
f. Removal and appointment of company secretary
g. Alteration of business objectives (Company's Memorandum and Articles of Association.
h. Change of registered address
i. Addition or removal of shareholders
j. Addition of proprietors
k. Re-registration/Conversion of business name to limited liability company

Annual Returns:

Filing of annual returns is an annual event in every registered business entity. It is an obligation imposed by the Law (Companies and Allied Matters Act). In line with the words, "annual returns" means that you need to make certain returns to the Corporate Affairs Commission annually. All registered businesses are expected to file annual returns every year except the year of their registration. If you operate as a business name, you are expected to file your annual returns on or before the 30th day of June every year following your business name registration.

If your brand is an incorporated company, you have to file your first annual returns within 18months of incorporation and subsequently within 12 (twelve) months. If you operate a limited liability partnership, you are expected to file your annual returns within 60days of closure of the financial year.

An up-to-date annual return is a requirement to commence other post-incorporation matters that may arise in your business. Failure to file your annual returns may attract penalty for each year the return was not filed.

Change of Company/Business name:

Your company, partnership or business name is identified by its name. Your brand name is what first distinguishes your company from another before the products are being considered. It is highly recommended that your corporate name should be simple, self-expressive and descriptive of your business where possible. Although that may not be desirable where your business is registered to do multiple things across different industries. The fact that your corporate name has been registered does not stop you from changing the name if you have to. The name can be changed at any time after registration and such changes will not affect the objectives of the company or its shareholding structure and other details.

If you or the board of your incorporated company (precisely limited liability company) decides to change the company's name, the board of the company is to meet to deliberate on a choice name and thereafter conduct a name search for the availability of the proposed new name. You may then proceed to have it reserved for your use. Upon the reservation of the name, your company is to pass a resolution to change the company's name to the approved name. The Corporate Affairs Commission is to be notified within 15 days of the passing of the resolution for a name change. You would also need to submit an application to the Corporate Affairs Commission requesting for a change of the company name to the reserved name. Once the request is approved, the old certificate which bears the old name is to be returned to the Corporate Affairs Commission and a new certificate reflecting the new name will be issued. In a similar vein, the company's name on its Memorandum and Articles of

Association is to be changed to the new name and stamped at the FIRS stamp duty office. The Corporate Affairs Commission will usually not allow any changes in a company's records without the company's annual returns being up to date.

Where the change is in a business name, you would have to first reserve the new name. Once approved, you can make an application to the Corporate Affairs Commission for name change alongside evidence of up-to-date annual returns and original certificate bearing the old name.

Removal or addition of Director

Your company is mandated by the provisions of the law to have at least two directors, except your company is a small company which can have a sole director. This is, therefore, to say that while the number can be more than two, it should not go below two for large companies and public companies.

Following the incorporation of your company, there may be a reason to either remove a director or appoint a director. Whichever is applicable, your company has a duty to notify the Corporate Affairs Commission (CAC) of the decision to either remove or appoint a new director by completing the applicable form, attach the company resolution, resignation letter where applicable, the appointment letter, a copy of means of Identification where applicable and evidence of up-to-date filing of your company's annual returns. You will need to submit all at the Corporate Affairs Commission office within 14 days of the decision else penalty will be charged for late notification.

Removal and appointment of company secretary

The 1990 Companies and Allied Matters Act mandates all companies to have a company secretary, at no time should a company be without a secretary. The 2020 Companies and Allied Matters Act however exempts small companies from the mandatory need to have a company secretary. Where there is a need to remove your company's secretary, the company is expected to notify the Corporate Affairs Commission of such removal and appoint another to replace the removed secretary.

To effectively do this, the company is to complete the applicable CAC Form, attach the resolution and evidence of up-to-date filing of the company's annual returns and submit at the CAC office.

Alteration of Business Objectives.

An Incorporated company can do businesses that are stated in its Memorandum of Association. The directors of a company will be sanctioned where a company is engaged in activities specifically prohibited by the Memorandum and Articles of Association. To avoid these sanctions and to specify the scope of your company's business, the law permits you to adjust the objectives of the company.

To add to or remove from your company's objectives, a resolution is to be passed stating the clauses to be added or removed.

The Memorandum and Articles of Association (MEMART) will also need to be altered accordingly to reflect the changes after which document is restamped at the stamp duty office of the Federal Inland Revenue Service.

The resolution and altered MEMART is to be submitted to the Corporate Affairs Commission alongside evidence of up-to-date filing of the company's annual returns after 15days following the expiration of 28days of stamping of the MEMART at the Stamp Duty office.

Change of registered address

The business address is one of the details required at the point of registering your company. Some businesses retain their home address as the registered address while some make use of leased premises. The business address used at the registration stage may be a temporary address which may need to be changed following the registration.

Your business is expected to have an accessible business address, as it serves the purpose of receiving correspondences from government organisations and individuals. A registered business address is an important detail of a business which should subsist and be accessible as the business continues to remain a going concern.

For you to change your company's registered address, you will need to fill the applicable CAC Form. If the subject is an incorporated company, you will need to prepare and attach board resolution approving the change of address, attach the evidence of up-to-date filing of the company's annual returns and present all for filing at the CAC office within 14 days of the passing of the resolution.

Addition or removal of shareholders

One of the questions we usually ask clients at the point of registering their companies is whether or not the shares are to be allotted fully or in part such that new shareholders can be added later.

Under the defunct law, you are required to issue at least 25% of your company's share capital at the point of incorporation. That way, some shares can be left un-allotted while incorporating the company. Where a company has allotted all its shares and desire to bring in new shareholders, it might have to increase its share capital or otherwise recapitalise.

Conversely, the extant law changed the 25% issued shares rule and replaced it with a requirement for the entire share capital to be fully issued at the time of registration.

The new law does not remove a company's right to increase its share capital whenever it needs to. Although, the process of increasing issued shares might be cumbersome, the mischief that the law seeks to cure is that of payments made for stamp duty on total shares when in fact it is not all shares that are issued.

When a decision is therefore made to bring on board new

shareholders, the company is to pass a resolution stating details of the new shareholder and the shareholding, where it is by way of transfer, a transfer document is to be prepared between the old and the new shareholders, the applicable Corporate Affairs Commission form is to be duly completed and evidence of up-to-date filing of the company's annual returns is to be submitted alongside to the Corporate Affairs Commission office within 14 days where it is by way of transfer of shares or 15 days where it is a new allotment.

Addition/Removal of Partners of a registered Limited Liability Partnership

We earlier discussed limited liability partnership business in chapter one. The entity is not without obligations to be performed upon registration. Every limited liability partnership is mandated to at all times have at least two designate partners.

Where you commence your business under this structure and the total number of partners go below two for a period of 6 (six) months, the only partner carrying on the business of the partnership for that period will be solely and personally liable for the liabilities incurred during those months.

Also, where any partner exits the partnership, the designated partners are to notify the commission (CAC) within 30 days of the exit. This 30 days' notice window also applies where there is a change in any of the particulars of the partners, such as name or address.

Like an incorporated company, a limited liability partnership makes decisions by way of resolution which is to be filed at the Corporate Affairs Commission office. Where there is a decision to change the registered address of the partnership, the designated partners are to notify the commission within 14 (fourteen) days of the change, else it will not take effect. Failure to do this leaves all partners liable for each day the commission is not notified of the change of address.

Addition of Proprietors

Your business can be registered with just you as the sole owner, especially with the provision of one-man company in the new Companies and Allied Matters Act. A sole business owner now has an option of either registering a business name or incorporating a company. Where you opt for business name registration and find a partner to co-own the business, the available option is to add the new partner as a proprietor by filing the addition at the Corporate Affairs Commission office after completing the necessary documents for addition of proprietor and attaching evidence of up-to-date filed annual returns. You have a duty to notify the Corporate Affairs Commission within 28days from the date the addition of your new partner is being executed.

Re-registration/Conversion of Business name to Limited Liability Company

Your registered business name can be re-registered as an Incorporated company with the same name but with the addition of the word "LTD" or "Limited". This can be done in two ways; it can either be a dissolution of the business name or an application for consent to use the name as a limited liability company (LTD). Where the former is preferred, you are to write the Commission notifying it of your intention to cease doing business in the already registered name, you are to attach the original certificate given to you and the attached business name form.

Once your letter is received and sanctioned by the Commission, the name will be available for use for the company to be incorporated because it will be removed from the registered business.

Where the latter option is preferred, you will need to prepare a letter seeking the Commission's consent to use the registered business name in registering a Limited. The letter should state that the Applicant is the proprietor of the business and that the Applicant desires to incorporate an LTD with the name. Once the consent is obtained you can commence company registration.

In conclusion, a post-incorporation decision not duly filed at the Corporate Affairs Commission office and approved by the commission is not recognised except there is full compliance in law. For example, where your company appoints a new director and secretary who are in active service of the company, any document executed by such director or secretary will not be recognised as the law will only recognise a director on record.

EFFECT OF NON-COMPLIANCE

The Corporate Affairs Commission disclosed some years back that it delisted 40,000 registered businesses from its database between October 2017 and October 2019. This was carried out to ensure that only the names of active registered businesses remain in the Commission's database.

Some time ago, in one of our training sessions for entrepreneurs, a participant asked the following question:

"Since the Corporate Affairs Commission, unlike the FIRS, does not send demand notices to businesses that are not complying, why then should a business be CAC-compliant?"

Compliance with Post-incorporation filings not only gives the commission up-to-date information about your business but also an evidence that your business remains a going concern which the public can transact with without any shadow of doubt- especially where a search is done on the status of the company at the Corporate Affairs Commission.

The commission is empowered by law to remove the name of dormant companies from its register when it has reasonable cause to believe that such registered entity is not in operation.

When can the Commission have reasonable cause to believe that your business is dormant?

The Act does not specifically give a list of conditions or incidents for removing a registered name. The word 'reasonable cause' was used but what conditions will then be considered as a reasonable cause or when can the Commission form an opinion or believe that you no longer carry on business activities? Best way to form an opinion is when the records of the Commission shows 'nil' for expected post-incorporation filings, especially annual returns which are to be filed every year.

One of the incidences of registration is that once your name is registered by the Commission, there is a restriction on the use of such name by another person, except with your consent. If the Commission believes that your company is dormant, it reserves the right to strike the name off the register, after which a person can register such name after the expiration of the grace period for relisting an already removed name.

Note that the notification to you of the commencement of removal of your business name by the commission will be delivered to the address in your CAC records, which is to say that you can only receive this notice if your business is still being carried on in the same address with which the business was registered. This is another reason you are mandated to notify the Commission of a change in your address. In other words, if your business is still a going concern, the Commission would not be aware of the state of your business if it is being carried on in an address unknown to the Commission.

Can a removed name be relisted?

Where your registered name has been removed, you can apply to the court at any time before the expiration of 20 years from the publication of the notice of removal, for an order restoring the company to the register; and if the court is satisfied that, at the time of the striking off, the company was carrying on business or in operation, the court may order the name of the company to be restored to the record.

BUSINESS TAXATION
IN NIGERIA

By way of definition, tax includes any duty, levy or revenue accruable to the government in full or in part by way of law. Tax compliance entails keeping proper records, preparing tax returns, filings, and payment of taxes. Breach of tax compliance attracts severe consequences which may be in the form of interest, penalties, and imprisonment (people do not only get imprisoned for criminal acts, hence the need for compliance).

Payment of tax is one aspect that most business owners try to avoid. A writer once wrote that when you become a small business owner, you acquire responsibility for making tax payments that you did not have as an employee. What do you think about this assertion?

When you make money from your business, irrespective of the

size or economic strength of your business, you have to pay income tax (either as Personal Income Tax or Company Income Tax).

Registering a business name, company or Non-Governmental Organisation (NGO) is not an end in itself.

In our years of registering various kinds of businesses for clients, we have discovered that once a certificate of registration with the Corporate Affairs Commission is presented to clients, they often back out thinking that they are done with compliance needs that affect their businesses.

This, however, is not the true position because under the law, there is an additional obligation, the need to process a unique tax identification number (TIN - an identification number given to all businesses and individuals to enable them remit their taxes to the appropriate government authority) thereafter. It helps you keep all records of payments made to the government as taxation fees through government tax offices spread across the country.

Tax Identification Number

The first step to becoming tax compliant is to apply for your Business or Company's Tax Identification Number. This number is generated electronically and usually assigned to the particular business name, company or individual that applied for it. The 2019 Finance Act mandates banks and other financial institutions to include the production of Tax Identification Number (TIN) as a precondition to opening a new business account or operating an existing business account. The requirement for TIN is contained in both the Personal Income Tax Act and The Companies Income Tax Act. It is no news that individuals now open and operate corporate/business accounts for their business names upon registration with the Corporate Affairs Commission. It should therefore be noted that the TIN requirement is mandatory for individual business operations and bank opening for such business purposes.

It is worthy of note that without a TIN, your business will not be able to have a corporate account in its registered name, this will limit you from doing business in the long run especially when the business has expanded. This is because most organised businesses would not want to ordinarily transact with any business that does not have its corporate account.

It is an offence to commence your business without obtaining a TIN. When you commence business without obtaining your TIN, you will be in default for the period you carried on business without registration and may also be sanctioned. In Nigeria, there is a constitutional duty to pay tax promptly. All persons in employment, individuals in business, including non-residents who derive income from Nigeria, as well as companies that operate in Nigeria, are liable to pay tax.

Taxes are assessed at a rate on profits, income rent premiums, interests, benefits, any fees, dues or allowances of companies and businesses and persons.

WHO IS RESPONSIBLE FOR COLLECTING AND RECEIVING TAXES IN NIGERIA?

The first thing to note is the appropriate authority to collect and receive tax. The Federal Government collects tax for all federal government establishments, corporate bodies and other statutory provided activities. Company income tax is payable only to the federal government.

The State Government collects income tax of individuals and unincorporated entities; the various local government councils are only allowed to collect rates and levies and not personal income tax. Examples of taxes and levies to be collected by the Local Government are shops and kiosks rates, market taxes, and levies excluding any market where State finance is involved, signboard, and advertisement permit fees, amongst others.

BASIC TAXES APPLICABLE IN NIGERIA

There is no single one-off form of taxation that covers all the taxes payable in Nigeria, the taxes vary and would usually depend on the circumstances and activities surrounding the payment of the taxes, the sector or industry of operation of the payer, the status of the payer and so on.

The following are the taxes that are payable in Nigeria:

1. Personal income tax
2. Value-added tax
3. Company income tax
4. Withholding tax
5. Capital gains tax
6. Education tax

There are also industry specific taxes (an example is petroleum tax for companies involved in the drilling of oil wells or other related matters) but the above are the most applicable to businesses generally.

Personal Income Tax

For those in paid employment, employers are to withhold a part of employees' salary as tax. All the amounts that are deducted ought to be remitted to the tax authority of the State where the staff resides.

The income of unincorporated entities and that of business name owners are regarded as personal income of the owners and are therefore assessed under personal income tax.

Every business name owner is also expected to have a Tax Identification Number (TIN).

In Lagos, it is called Payer's Identification Number (Payer's ID). If your business involves import and export, you may wish to apply for TIN at the FIRS. The law allows some deductions to be made on your profits before assessing tax on what is left. Tax will only be assessed on what is left after deducting the amount allowed to be deducted under the law.

Value Added Tax

Every business in Nigeria (whether an incorporated company, sole proprietorship or partnership) is required to be an agent of the Federal Government to collect and remit VAT (Value Added

Tax). Prior to the 2019 Finance Act, VAT was charged at a rate of 5% on goods and services not exempted from VAT charges. The 2019 Act introduced an increase from 5% to 7.5% which is a 50% increase. However, some classes of business might not have to deal with VAT in their business operation.

The old VAT law mandated all suppliers of goods and services to charge 5% as VAT for every supply of goods and services irrespective of the size of business or the class of goods and services except on goods and services expressly exempted from VAT.

The new Act introduced THRESHOLDS by classifying businesses in levels, thereby protecting the most vulnerable from exposure to being a VAT collection agent. Under the new VAT regime, only a business owner who, in the course of business, has made taxable supplies or expects to make taxable supplies to the value of Twenty Five Million Naira either singularly or cumulatively, is liable to remit VAT to the commission on or before the 21st day of every month in which the threshold is achieved.

If your business does not make a total supply to the value of Twenty Five Million Naira, you are exempted from charging and remitting VAT to FIRS. You are also exempted from registering your business with FIRS for VAT purposes and consequently exempted from penalty for not registering, penalty for not charging VAT on your invoice, penalty for not filing VAT returns and penalty for late filing.

The 2019 Act increased and provided specific details of items exempted from VAT, for example services of microfinance banks are now expressly exempted from VAT. As such, that industry will be more attractive to investors who are interested in micro-banking and business owners can take advantage of benefiting from VAT free transactions.

The VAT law also expanded the definition of goods exempted from VAT such as food items that are VAT free. For instance, locally produced sanitary towels and tuition for primary, secondary, and tertiary institutions have been added to the list of goods and services exempted from VAT.

All business owners (business name owners and Incorporated Companies) ought to register for VAT from the commencement of business operations. Failure to register with FIRS is punishable with a penalty of NGN 50,000 for the first month and NGN 25,000 for each subsequent month in which the failure continues. When you hit the Twenty Five Million threshold, you are to commence the inclusion of 7.5% of the total goods and services supplied as VAT on your invoices when sending to your clients/customers.

When you receive payment, the VAT should be remitted to the Federal Inland Revenue Service (FIRS) on or before the 21st day of the month following the month the goods or services were sold. For example, VAT collected from 1st - 31st January should be remitted on or before 21st February.

The amendment of the Finance Act has brought about some changes in the companies that are permitted to remit VAT. This is because of the thresholds that have been created under the Finance Act based on the annual income of various companies.

Withholding Tax

This is tax deducted at source to bring the taxpayer within the tax net. The name, as it connotes, implies that the law permits a person to withhold a part of the sum of money, which the person should ordinarily pay to another, as a tax to be remitted either to the State or Federal Government. It is tax withheld or deducted from the income due to the recipient.

Where the transaction involves individuals, a group of individuals or an unincorporated entity, it is to be paid to the State Government and where it is an incorporated company, it is remitted to the Federal Government. The essence of withholding tax is to curb tax evasion by ensuring everybody within the tax net pays tax via source deduction.

Companies Income Tax

Every profit-oriented company is liable to be assessed for company income tax, except petroleum companies. This tax does not apply to those that carry on business under a registered business name. Companies Taxation is governed by the Companies Income Tax Act.

One of the laudable provisions of the Finance Act is that it groups companies according to their financial capacity and then uses that standard to establish company income tax (CIT) obligations. The old tax law in its regressive nature imposed 30% of Companies Income as taxable profits, even though it had a provision that allowed manufacturing and agricultural businesses in their first 5-7 years to pay tax at a reduced rate of 20%. This incentive did not apply to start-ups, Small Enterprises and Medium-sized Companies; it placed all companies on the same pedestal.

The 2019 Finance Act which amends some provisions of the Companies Income Tax Act however introduces a new tax rate for companies which is progressive in nature and in line with the Federal Government of Nigeria's commitment to encourage growth and development of small companies thereby projecting the goals of the umbrella of ease of doing business reforms. Companies have been classified into three for tax purposes. They are:

1. Small Companies: These are companies with an annual turnover that is not more than 25 million naira. They enjoy a complete exemption from paying companies income tax. They however must ensure that they promptly file nil returns for their company income tax returns so as to avoid the chances of being penalised.

2. Medium Sized Companies: These are companies with turnover above 25 million Naira but less than 100 million Naira. The required percentage payable as tax is 20%.

3. Large Companies: Every other company with annual gross turnover above 100 million Naira is considered to be a large company and is required to remit 30% as tax.

The obligations of companies exempted from Companies Income Tax is to promptly file their CIT returns every year, comply with other statutory duties such as tax registration, failure of which penalties will apply for non-compliance.

Small companies are exempted from registering, charging and filing VAT returns. While they are exempted from company income tax, the law provides for them to file (nil) company income returns. The rationale for this may not be unconnected with the need for FIRs to have access to companies' records to justify their status as a small company.

You therefore still have a duty to register for TIN because you have to file the company's annual returns every accounting year, and where your company files at a later date, penalties will be levied for late filing.

Notably too, businesses carried on in the digital space are now specifically covered under the tax laws, most especially companies that do not have a physical presence in Nigeria.

On a general note, the Act also provides for industry specific benefits. For example, Companies in Agricultural production now have a clearly defined tax incentive of 5 years which can be extended for another 3 years, subject to satisfactory performance of such business.

The way to go is to apply to the appropriate authority for tax exemption (i.e. apply to Nigeria Investment Promotion Council through the office of the Minister of Industry, Trade and Investment).

Companies income tax is assessed at the rate of 0% for small-sized companies, 20% for medium sized Companies and 30% for large companies on profits for the accounting year ending in the year preceding assessment and paid annually.

Note also that the law allows some deductions while calculating your tax. This is to say a company's tax is 0%, 20%, 30% (as the case may be) of the profit, minus allowable deductions. Examples are cost of sale, gross profit, selling and distribution expenses, salaries, power, rent on land and building used for business, repairs and maintenance incurred on the business, legal expenses, or expenses wholly, reasonably, exclusively and necessarily incurred for the business, salaries and wages, etc.

Education Tax

This tax is imposed on every company at the rate of 2% of the assessable profit for each year of assessment. Due for payment within 60 days of service of an assessment notice from the FIRS. (You can also do a self-assessment by computing 2% from your taxable income, most companies pay alongside their Company's income tax).

Capital Gains Tax

This is a tax on the profit made from the sale of assets. It is assessed at a rate of 10% on the profit realised from the disposal of any form of asset. It is 10% of the sale of an asset minus deductible sum (e.g. initial cost price, cost of maintenance; reasonable expenses are allowed to be deducted from the amount you sold the asset).

Common breaches of Tax to avoid.

With the content of preceding paragraphs in this module, we hope you are better informed on various tax provisions as they relate to your business. Below are common breaches of tax compliance to avoid:

- Failure to register and obtain a TIN.

- Failure to keep proper business records.

- Failure to prepare and file tax returns on or before the due date.

- Failure to pay correct tax computed by you on or before the due date.

- Engaging the services of touts to transact tax business on your behalf.

- Engaging in tax evasion practices.

- Transacting business without a valid TIN.

- Transacting business without genuine Tax Clearance Certificate (TCC).

- Failure to charge, withhold and remit WHT, PAYE and VAT to FIRS.

- Allowing another person/company to use your TIN for the purpose of seeking a contract award.

- Payment of a particular tax type into the wrong account. E.g. VAT into CIT.

In conclusion, as a business owner, you are enjoined to carefully arrange your business affairs in line with the Tax Acts, you are also enjoined to seek counsel from professionals on how best you can comply with the tax laws and its effect on your business.